MW00965641

CEO Guide to Doing Business in Asia: Singapore, Malaysia and Indonesia

By Ade Asefeso MCIPS MBA

Second Edition

ISBN-13: 978-1499783902

ISBN-10: 1499783906

Publisher: AA Global Sourcing Ltd
Website: http://www.aaglobalsourcing.com

Table of Contents

4

Other Titles in the Doing Business in Asia Series:

CEO Guide to Doing Business in
Asia
(Taiwan, Hong Kong and Macao)

CEO Guide to Doing Business in
Asia
(Thailand, Vietnam and Philippines)

Disclaimer

This publication is designed to provide competent and reliable information regarding the subject matter covered. However, it is sold with the understanding that the author and publisher are not engaged in rendering professional advice. The authors and publishers specifically disclaim any liability that is incurred from the use or application of contents of this book.

If you purchased this book without a cover you should be aware that this book may have been stolen property and reported as "unsold and destroyed" to the publisher. In this case neither the author nor the publisher has received any payment for this "stripped book."

Dedication

To my family and friends who seems to have been sent here to teach me something about who I am supposed to be. They have nurtured me, challenged me, and even opposed me…. But at every juncture has taught me!

This book is dedicated to my lovely boys, Thomas, Michael and Karl. Teaching them to manage their finance will give them the lives they deserve. They have taught me more about life, presence, and energy management than anything I have done in my life.

Part 1: CEO Guide to Doing Business in Singapore

Chapter 1: Introduction

Are you a CEO, consultant, or entrepreneur interested in entering or expanding your activity in the Singapore market?

Then this book is for you!

The main objective of this book is to provide you with basic knowledge about Singapore; an overview of its economy, business culture, potential opportunities and an introduction to other relevant issues. Novice exporters, in particular will find this book a useful starting point.

Singapore is a small but wealthy city-state, occupying a strategically vital location at the southernmost tip of Peninsular Malaysia, where major sea lanes between east and west converge. Singapore's historic role as trans-shipment centre for the region has traditionally created opportunities across a broad spectrum of sectors. This globally connected, multi-cultural and cosmopolitan city state offers a conducive environment, especially to creative and knowledge-driven businesses.

Singapore is a model of economic development. From independence in 1965, it achieved almost uninterrupted growth averaging nearly 8% per annum for over three decades. By the 1990s, it had GDP per capita levels similar to many OECD countries and was acknowledged widely as one of Asia's 'tigers'. The contrast between Singapore and some of its regional neighbours is all the more striking given its size and lack of natural resources.

However, given the openness of its economy (Singapore trades over 350% of its GDP), it was the first country in Asia to fall into recession, after three consecutive quarters of contraction in 2008. GDP growth for 2008 came in at 1.1% and provisional figures for 2009 indicate a contraction of 2.1%. The announcement of S$20.5 billion stimulus package in the 2009 Budget, and a 2010 Budget focusing on improving productivity by 2% to 3% a year over the next decade, has enabled the Government to raise its growth forecast for the economy for 2010 to between 4.5 to 6.5%.

Chapter 2: Opportunities in Singapore

Global businesses will find it advantageous to site their headquarters in Singapore. Companies situating their headquarters in Singapore will benefit from Singapore's network of over 50 comprehensive Double Taxation Avoidance Agreements, 35 Investment Guarantee Agreements and many free trade agreements. Singapore's FTAs have been instrumental in helping Singapore-based businesses strengthen cross-border trade by eliminating or reducing import tariff rates, providing preferential access to services sectors, easing investment rules, improving intellectual property regulations, and opening government procurement opportunities. These FTAs have enabled Singapore to establish a network to countries that contribute at least 60% of global GDP. Companies can rely on protection of their ideas and innovations through Singapore's rigorous enforcement of its strong intellectual property laws.

Singapore is a leading provider of services such as international banking, trade finance, maritime finance, insurance, treasury operations, and asset and wealth management within the region.

Singapore is also fast emerging as an optimal destination for centralisation of services or "shared services". Centralising activities such as IT, finance and logistics, offers benefits such as lower operating costs, consistent services levels and enhanced productivity.

There are opportunities for British exports in almost all commercial sectors, in particular:
1. Advanced Engineering
2. Biomedical Sciences
3. Creative Industries
4. Education and Training
5. Environment
6. Financial Services
7. Infrastructure Development
8. Oil & Gas

Singapore is the UK's largest trading partner in South-East Asia and one of its largest export markets outside Europe. UK exports of goods and services were worth £5.7bn in 2007, making it the UK's 14th largest export market. The UK is also the largest investor in Singapore with over 700 UK companies based in Singapore. The UK and Singapore have signed Double Taxation and Investment Protection agreements. In addition, the EU will open negotiations for a free trade agreement (FTA) with Singapore in March 2010, which, once signed, should help increase trade even further.

Chapter 3: Economic and Political Overview

The building blocks of Singapore's economy, post-independence, were trade, manufacturing, shipbuilding, ship repair and oil refining. Singapore is the world's busiest port by container volume and tonnage and its refineries make it one of the largest oil-refining centres in Asia. As the economy matured and a more highly skilled workforce developed, financial and business services, telecommunications, electronics and professional services transformed Singapore into the regional centre of operations and a manufacturing base for over 7,000 multinational companies across a broad spectrum of industries.

Typical of all sectors in the nineties, manufacturing moved up the value chain, with electronics commanding a 30% global share of hard disk drive output, for example. In response to global competition, including lower manufacturing costs in neighbouring countries, Singapore shifted the focus to higher value-added services catering to a global knowledge-based economy. The attention is now on research and development, info-communication, e-business, media, digital entertainment and life sciences.

Singapore increasingly serves as a hub for South East Asia across an extensive range of financial and business services. Both its port and airport are world class, regularly winning industry awards and offering excellent connectivity for shipping and airlines. Singapore's economy remains fundamentally strong and has rebounded with confidence.

Singapore is a multinational island city with a population of just under 5 million. It is a prosperous, modern and clean country. The diverse population of Singapore, consisting mainly of Chinese, Malay and Indians, does not possess one single dominant national identity. Drawing on a variety of traditions, different ethnic groups all consider themselves important parts of the diverse society of Singapore.

Singapore's population consists of 77% of Chinese origin, 14% Malay, 8% Indian and 1% others. Expatriates and foreign workers make up about 1.5m of the population which included around 26,800 British residents. Population density is amongst the highest in the world at around 6,100 per km2. To do business successfully in Singapore, an understanding of the population's different cultural traditions and background is critical.

In the Singapore Government 2010 budget announcement, focus is given on Productivity, and is seeking to gradually reduce Singapore dependence on foreign workers.

Singapore is a republic within the Commonwealth. It has an elected President. The People's Action Party (PAP) has governed Singapore since internal self-government in 1959. Lee Kuan Yew (LKY), who led the country since 1959, stood down as Prime Minister in 1990. He was succeeded by Goh Chok Tong, who stood down himself in 2004, to be succeeded in turn by the current Prime Minister, Lee Hsien Loong, LKY's son.

LKY is, however, still a serving member of the Cabinet and continues to exert influence from his position as "Minister Mentor" in the Prime Minister's Office. Goh Chok Tong continues to serve in the Cabinet as "Senior Minister". Of the 94 MPs in the unicameral Parliament, the PAP holds 82 of 84 elected seats; one non-constituency MP and nine nominated MPs make up the remainder.

Chapter 4: Getting there and advice about your Stay

By Air

As an international crossroads in South East Asia, Singapore is within easy reach of all key points in the region. Upon arrival, your flight will land at Changi Airport, which is recognised as one of the best airports in the world, with over 80 airlines serving 200 cities in 60 countries. Changi Airport is located in the east of Singapore. There are regular daily flights between the UK and Singapore.

By Sea

Singapore claims to be the world's busiest port. Passenger lines serve Singapore from Europe, Australia, USA, India and Hong Kong. Ships either dock at the Harbour Front or anchor in the main harbour with a launch service to shore.

By Train

Singapore is connected by rail to Malaysia. Three fully air-conditioned express trains make the trip daily between Singapore (Tanjong Pagar Railway Station) and Kuala Lumpur (Keretapi Tanah Melayu station). The journey takes 7-8 hours and costs between S$34-S$68 one-way (depending on class of travel).

By Road

It takes approximately 5 hours to drive by taxi or private car from Kuala Lumpur to Singapore on the North-South Highway. There are two crossings to Malaysia, the causeway (S$1.20 toll) to Johor Bahru and the newer Tuas Second Link (S$4.60 toll). Long distance bus companies also operate between Singapore and Kuala Lumpur costing between S$30 – S$40 one way.

Your stay

Getting around Singapore is effortless: the public transportation system is amongst the best in the world and taxis are reasonably priced. Very few visitors rent cars. The Singapore Tourism Board website http://www.stb.gov.sg and the public transport web page http://www.publictransport.sg provide further information to help you plan your trip.

Singapore has strict laws against littering and is subject to between S$1,000 to S$2,000 fine and a stint of corrective work order cleaning a public place for repeat offenders. The import, sale and possession of chewing gum is prohibited in Singapore.

Chapter 5: What Companies should consider when Doing Business in Singapore

Singapore is an international financial centre and the trading hub for the region. Its population is cosmopolitan, well educated and well travelled. It is generally an easy place to do business and what would be considered normal business behaviour in the UK will almost invariably be acceptable in Singapore.

UK Businesses are advised to research the market and the companies they intend to contact. Singapore has high internet penetration and much information is readily available on government and corporate websites. You should plan your visit, organising appointments before departure. Follow up with telephone calls on arrival to confirm availability. It is advisable to arrange a market discussion with the relevant Senior Trade & Investment Officer at the High Commission. However, UK businesses must not expect to do businesses immediately or necessarily on the first visit to Singapore.

Singapore is in some ways more conservative than the UK; good manners and more formal forms of address are essential. When making initial contact with a business, try to aim high; you may end up being passed on to a subordinate but if you start lower down the company structure it can prove difficult to gain access to senior decision makers.

Although Singapore is a price sensitive market, the current exchange rate makes UK products and services more attractive. Singapore is also an excellent test-bed for the wider Asia Pacific region, the growth market of the future.

Gateways/Locations – Key areas for business

Thanks to its geographical location, its port, airport and deregulated telecommunications, Singapore is a regional centre for practically every commercial activity: transhipment, warehousing, distribution, procurement, financial and business services to name some of the most important.

The links Singapore's Chinese business community has with its counterparts in the region have reinforced these advantages. Trading links with Malaysia and Indonesia are strong and established.

The emerging markets of China, Indochina and India (Singapore has a significant Indian community), have also become key areas of activity. Most of the multinational corporations based here use Singapore as their regional HQ, some of which cover the Indian sub-continent, Japan, China and Australasia.

Market entry and start up considerations

Singapore has an excellent range of capable agents, representatives and potential partners who have the expertise and connections to enable them to penetrate local and regional markets. The choice of direct selling, an informal agency agreement, or a formal one will depend on the circumstances. Direct selling is advised where potential customers are few; a formal agency agreement is preferable where it is important to commit an agent to active promotion.

Chapter 6: Singapore Key Facts

Singapore is essentially a free port and very few foods are dutiable or under control. Import duties are levied on such items as alcohol, tobacco, petroleum products, motor vehicles and certain products that are manufactured, or are to be manufactured in Singapore (e.g. cosmetics and furniture). Controlled items include animals, meat products, plants, arms, explosives, medicines, pharmaceuticals, films and telecommunications equipment. The duty rates applicable are either a percentage of the value of the goods or a specified amount per unit of quantity.

Enquiries on custom matters, such as valuation, classification, documentary requirements and clearance procedures, can be made to the Singapore Customs (http://www.customs.gov.sg).

Company law in Singapore is very similar to that in the UK. There is no restriction on the type of business that may be set up, but some, such as financial services companies, chemical producers and motor manufacturers have to apply for special licences from the government/ Registrar of Manufacturers. All businesses must be registered with the Accounting & Corporate Regulatory Authority (ACRA) (http://www.acra.gov.sg). It is advisable to employ the services of a firm of solicitors or accountants to attend to the formalities of registering a company.

Singapore has an open and transparent regime of acquiring tenders. The vast majority of public sector invitations for quotations and tenders are posted on the Singapore government's one-stop e-procurement portal, GeBIZ (http://www.gebiz.gov.sg). Suppliers can search for government procurement opportunities, download tender documents, and submit their bids online.

Singapore has a talented workforce that is ranked highly for productivity, work attitude and technical skills. Workers speak English proficiently and are constantly looking to upgrade their skills and knowledge. A host of worker-training and scholarship programmes makes this possible.

For further information on Singapore's labour market, employment laws, recruitment services, and worker training and staff development schemes please see the EnterpriseOne website (http://www.business.gov.sg).

Singapore welcomes specialist foreign talent. On average, it takes less than two weeks to get employment passes for foreign staff. If you require a specialist or manager to come to Singapore for a short-term project, approval can be issued in around three working days. Full details of the various kinds of employment passes, as well as dependency passes for family members, are available at the Ministry of Manpower website (http://www.mom.gov.sg).

Chapter 7: Singapore Key Regulations

Documentation

Import /export permits are required from the Singapore Customs. The process of trade documents is handled electronically through TradeNet (www.tradenet.gov.sg), an electronic data interchange system implemented by Singapore Customs. Invoices must show an accurate description of the goods, quantity or weight, the country of origin, CIF value and commission/discount. Bills of Lading may be made out "To Order". Metric units for used for weights and measures.

For import of all goods (including controlled and non-controlled items) into Singapore, businesses are required to:
1. Obtain an IN Permit through TradeNet® before goods are imported into Singapore, and
2. Pay the duty and/or Goods and Services Tax (GST) due at the prevailing rate at the time of importation.

Some countries subject certain high-technology items to export control. In such cases, the exporter may ask the Singapore importer to provide an Import Certificate and Delivery Verification (ICDV) so that the exporter can seek approval from his government authority to export these items. Items covered by an

ICDV must be imported directly in Singapore and are not to be diverted to other countries. Importers can apply for an ICDV from Singapore Customs.

Labelling and Packaging Regulations

Some of the areas where labelling regulations are in force include food, medicines and cosmetics. Labelling of food products is governed by the Sale of Food Act. This requires all pre-packed food to indicate the name, ingredients, permitted colouring, quantity of contents, name and address of local manufacturer or importer and the expiry date of the product. Companies seeking further information can visit the Agri-Food & Veterinary Authority of Singapore (http://www.ava.gov.sg).

Packaging and labelling requirements for medicinal products are laid down in the Medicines Act. In general, a medicinal product in a container or package should not be labelled or marked in a way to falsely describe the product or mislead as to the nature or quality of the product or its uses and effects. Enquiries can be addressed to the Centre for Drug Administration, Pharmacovigilance, Communications & Research Division, Health Sciences Authority (http://www.hsa.gov.sg).

Information on both Acts covering food and medicine are available on publications published by the SNP Corporation (http://www.snpcorp.com).

Getting your Goods to the Market

As an exporter of goods you will need to develop an understanding of various issues such as the legal and regulatory requirements your consignments have to comply with; paperwork involved; choosing the right mode of transport; protection for your goods; packaging; labelling; how freight forwarders can help you; rules for dangerous goods etc. Timely delivery of goods and services in Singapore is important. In some cases it may be worth considering employing a freight forwarder.

Standards and Technical Regulation

Singapore's voltage is 220-240 volts AC, 50 cycles per second. The use of a transformer can convert the voltage to 110-120 volts AC, 60 cycles per second. The power plugs used in Singapore are of the 3-pin, square-shaped type, similar to the UK.

International Direct Dialing is available at the General Post Office and the Comcentre. IDD calls can be made from numerous phone card and credit card phones located at post offices and around the city area. Phone cards are sold at Singapore Telecom service outlets, post offices, convenience stores and some retail shops. A 20% levy is normally imposed on IDD calls made from hotels.

Intellectual Property Rights

The Intellectual Property Office of Singapore (IPOS) is the lead government agency that advises on and

31

administers intellectual property (IP) laws, promotes IP awareness and provides the infrastructure to facilitate the development of IP in Singapore. As IP regulator and policy advisor, IPOS is committed to maintaining a robust and pro-business IP regime for the protection and commercial exploitation of IP.

Singapore has a fully Trade Related Aspects of Intellectual Property Rights (TRIPS)-compliant Intellectual Property Rights (IPR) legislative and administrative regime. It is also a signatory to a number of major international conventions. On the policy front, IPOS works with economic agencies and the IP business community to formulate and review IP policies and practices. An area of IPOS' work that has become increasingly important is in leading negotiations on IP issues in Singapore's growing network of Free Trade Agreements with other countries. Further details are available on the IPOS website (http://ipos.gov.sg).

In the 2010 Budget, the Singapore Government has announced that it will be introducing a Productivity and Innovation Credit. The Credit will cover six activities along the innovation chain, including research and development done in Singapore; acquisition of intellectual property (IP); registration of IP and investments in design done in Singapore.

Chapter 8: Business Etiquette, Language and Culture

Language

Singapore is generally a straightforward place to do business and what would be considered normal business in the UK will almost invariably be acceptable in Singapore. There are four official languages in Singapore; English, Mandarin, Malay and Tamil.

English is the language of business and administration, and is widely spoken. Translation and interpreting services are usually available at hotel business centres, but these services are unlikely to be required. Most Singaporeans are bilingual and speak their mother tongue as well as English.

Meetings and Presentations

Visiting (or name) cards are an essential part of business protocol. They should be presented with both hands and with the name facing the recipient. No elaborate bowing is necessary in formal business meetings. A firm handshake will suffice. When addressing Chinese people the family name is given first. For example, Mr Lee Tsien Sam would be addressed as Mr Lee. When addressing Malay people the first of their two family names is used. Singaporean Indians use a variety of conventions so it is advisable to use the family name.

There are no restrictions or differences for female business travellers. Punctuality is important so effort should be made to arrive on time.

Normal business attire consists of dark trousers, long-sleeved shirts and ties for men, and blouses, skirts or trousers for women. Due to the hot and humid weather, jackets are not usually required. Appointments should be made at least two weeks in advance.

Negotiations

Singapore has a formal business culture with many rules of etiquette, which vary between the Chinese, Malay and Indian members of the population. Singaporeans are cautious and likely to make sure they are doing business with the right person. As a result, it is necessary to establish a good and genuine relation with a Singaporean counterpart to demonstrate your capabilities are good.

Personal relationships and networking are important elements of doing businesses in Singapore. Status and hierarchy are important in Singapore business culture, where companies have a top-down structure. Decisions are nearly always taken by the senior management and subordinates avoid directly questioning or criticising their superiors.

Small talk is common at the outset of meetings; you may be asked questions about your family or other personal details; this is usually not considered rude, and part of the getting-to-know you phase. Politely sidestep these if you do not wish to answer.

Chapter 9: Healthcare Opportunities in Singapore

Singapore's world class healthcare system, spanning both public and private healthcare services, was ranked the sixth most effective system in the world and the best in Asia by WHO in 2000. Its medical standards are among the highest in Asia and it is widely acknowledged as a regional centre for medical excellence.

Healthcare services, along with medical technology, biotechnology and pharmaceuticals, comprise Singapore's Biomedical Sciences Sector, which is now the second largest manufacturing component of the economy. The ongoing investment by both the public and private sectors offers a myriad of opportunities to participate in this dynamic industry's growth.

Healthcare in Singapore is offered by both the public and private sectors, with the former providing 20% of primary care and 80% of tertiary care, and the latter providing the rest.

Healthcare spend is 3.7% of the GDP, which is set to rise with the growth in ageing population. The government's aim is to continue to provide quality medical care, while maintaining costs and Singapore's edge as the leading provider of high technology medicine in the region.

Ministry of Health priorities

MOH's five priority programmes are: to improve the health of the elderly; strengthening the management of the main killer diseases; enhancing child health services; improving mental health care; and health promotion and disease prevention. Under the 2009 Budget, £2 billion was committed over 5 years to expand the healthcare infrastructure to include:

1. Development of new hospitals, medical centres, labs and redevelopment of older hospitals.
2. New community hospitals and nursing homes.
3. Boosting capabilities in treating chronic and age-related diseases.
4. Training healthcare professionals.
5. Enhancing capabilities for long-term care (rehabilitation, home care and palliative services)
6. An electronic health records system accessible across hospitals and polyclinics, and eventually to the community care sector.
7. Research and public health initiatives.

A £60 million fund was announced in December 2010, to rebuild 6 nursing homes that would be the model for the 60 or so current nursing homes.
In April 2011, MOH announced its plans for the next 5 years as

1. Build a general hospital in every region.
2. Match the best in the world in health outcomes.
3. Redevelop polyclinics.

4. Transform long term care.
5. Get Singaporeans to stay healthy.
6. Involve the community on healthcare activities.
7. Keep healthcare services affordable.

Under the 2011 Budget, £3.5 billion was allocated for a range of healthcare measures:
1. Upgrading of five polyclinics over 5 years at a cost of £25 million and to build a new polyclinic.
2. New Hospital in the north east, with a community hospital by 2020.
3. £60 million for Health Promotion Board, to promote a healthy lifestyle, up from £56 million in 2010.
4. New institute to teach and do research in geriatric care.
5. £100 million for charities and VWOs that run nursing homes, community hospital and other community care services (up by 50%).
6. Top priority for the next 5 – 10 years is to build up better long term care, with more and better quality community hospitals, nursing homes and home healthcare.

New technology and solutions Singapore is committed to promoting innovation to achieve improved patient care and clinical outcomes, along with improved cost and operational efficiencies. New methods of medical treatment are constantly being tested and introduced, and the universities, hospitals and the industry collaborate to research and develop new medical devices and solutions. Translational medicine from the bench to the bedside and better integration across agencies, disciplines and industry for better economic outcomes is the current focus of Singapore's Biomedical Sciences initiative.

Information Technology

There is increasing use of IT in training, administration and service provision. Both large and small hospitals are exploring full computerisation of the patient data records and link up of all activities from admission to discharge. A national electronic health record system was launched in 2010 with comprehensive coverage by 2014, for patients to move seamlessly from their polyclinics or GPs to public, private or community hospitals. Singapore is also exploring RFID technology and telemedicine, and is enhancing its position as a teleradiology hub.

Care of the Elderly

Singapore will have the world's 4th oldest population by 2050. The Government's policy is to encourage family and home based care over institutionalised care, with access to community based services, for the estimated 800,000 elderly Singaporeans by 2030. The aim is to reduce the burden on acute care hospitals and build community hospitals and nursing homes around three regional hospitals to provide high quality, low cost 'step down care facilities' for non-acute medical care and rehabilitation services.

Measures to provide a seamless, integrated long term care infrastructure for the rapidly ageing population include home aids, transport services, community care, home modification, and comprehensive training of health care workers.

Mental Health

£44 million was allocated in 2007 to build Singapore into a mentally resilient society, to build community based capabilities and networks, to develop multi-disciplinary programmes to detect and treat mental health problems early, and reintegrate and rehabilitate mental health patients into the community.

A further £17.5 million was set aside in 2009 to strengthen capabilities and for customised programmes for different age groups.

Education and Training

In view of the ongoing shortage of healthcare professionals, training and skills upgrading is high priority to maintain the quality and standards of healthcare delivery.

New Medical University

Singapore's second medical university, the Duke-NUS Medical School, a joint venture between Duke University, USA, and the National University of Singapore, was opened in 2009. Located at the Outram campus which houses various hospitals and specialist centres, its 5 year course is very research led, to produce clinician-scientists. The Outram Campus

Master Plan also includes plans for schools for nurses, and other professionals such as physiotherapists.

Singapore's third medical school, a joint venture between Nanyang Technological University (NTU) and Imperial College London, to leverage on their strengths in engineering and science, will open by 2013. The Lee Kong Chian School of Medicine will be patient centric, training doctors to provide holistic care, using technology to enhance comfort and convenience for patients.

New Hospitals

Singapore's healthcare infrastructure is continually enhanced to cater to changing demographics and healthcare needs. A new hospital in the north, the £250 million, 550 bedded Khoo Teck Puat Hospital was opened in 2010. A second 700 bedded multi-disciplinary hospital in the west, the Ng Teng Fong Hospital will be operational in 2014. A new general hospital in the north east is targeted for 2018.

Further expansion of the National University Hospital and its speciality centres are in progress. In addition, there is re-development of existing hospitals and speciality centres, and new community hospitals and nursing homes for comprehensive step down care.

In the private sector, there are two new state of the art hospitals under development to cater to the growing medical travel market, as well as a new cancer centre.

Medical Tourism

Singapore has traditionally attracted regional patients for the quality of its healthcare infrastructure, its clinical excellence and cutting edge medical technology. Doctors in Singapore have developed capabilities in complex procedures such as organ transplant, assisted reproduction, limb reattachment, separation of conjoined twins, stem cell therapies and the world's first umbilical cord transplant, among others. Many of its clinicians are key opinion leaders in the region.

In addition, patients can access innovative treatments from the progressive clinical research taking place in Singapore. This is facilitated by Singapore's growing status as a centre for biomedical research, clinical trials and new drug and medical devices development, with several international pharmaceutical and medical technology companies setting up their manufacturing and R&D bases in Singapore.

Renowned medical institution, John Hopkins operates a medical centre in Singapore, its first outside USA.

Singapore received around 680,000 foreign patients in 2009. The target is to attract one million patients by 2012, while continuing to invest in its healthcare infrastructure, patient experience, clinical excellence, medical technology, skills upgrading and training.

Chapter 10: Security Opportunities in Singapore

As Singapore has become more urbanised, its infrastructure has become more sophisticated, and its people more affluent, the requirement for more advanced and widespread security systems has grown. The various terrorism activities that happened after 11 September 2001 in New York have heightened Singapore's awareness of its vulnerability as a small island. Given the government imperative that Singapore maintains its regional importance, security systems have become an integral and increasingly important part of new and existing buildings. In a population of 5.1 million, overall total crime rate has decreased 0.4% to 32,968 in 2009 from 33,113 in 2008. This may not be sustainable as people suffering the effects of economic downturn may have to take desperate measures to return to crime and especially when both the Integrated Resorts have started operation since February 2010. The Singapore Authorities have made clear their intention to continue to lower crime rates by reinforcing very strict laws and unfailing enforcement; television promotion campaigns, and increasing media coverage of crime; there is also very high level of public support for the law.

Singapore, which has one of Asia's best-equipped militaries, has raised its national defence budget by 5.4 per cent, with the government planning to spend £6.04 billion on defence in the 2012 fiscal year, up from £5.5 billion the year before. Singapore's navy, army and air force will get £5.7 billion to buy and maintain military equipment, for the upkeep of camps and for payment of salaries.

A total budget of £1,646 million has been allocated to the Ministry of Home Affairs for various projects for FY 2012.

IT Security, especially companies with expertise in counter cyber attack work, as Singapore looks to further develop their cyber infrastructure is another area of potential opportunity.

Ministry of Defence (MINDEF)

The mission of MINDEF and the Singapore Armed Forces (SAF) is to enhance Singapore's peace and security through deterrence and diplomacy, and should these fail, to secure a swift and decisive victory over the aggressor.

A total budget of £6.04 billion has been allocated to MINDEF in FY2012 towards achieving this mission. MINDEF aims to achieve the following outcomes:
1. Singaporeans continue to enjoy a peaceful and secure environment.
2. Singapore continues to have unimpeded access to its air and sea lines of communication.
3. MINDEF and the SAF maintain good defence relations with an extensive network of countries in the region and beyond.

4. The SAF maintains a high state of operational readiness to deter and respond to any conventional or non-conventional threats to Singapore's security.
5. The SAF equips its servicemen with the necessary skills and knowledge to leverage on technologically advanced weapons and operational doctrines of modern warfare.

Ministry of Home Affairs (MHA)

The mission of MHA is to make Singapore safe and secure. Guided by Ministry Headquarters, the functions of preserving internal security, enforcing law and order, and protecting lives and property are carried out by seven departments. They are the Singapore Police Force (SPF), the Internal Security Department (ISD), the Singapore Civil Defence Force (SCDF), the Singapore Prison Service (SPS), the Central Narcotics Bureau (CNB), the Immigration & Checkpoints Authority (ICA) and Home Team Academy (HTA). A total budget of £1646 million has been allocated to MHA in FY2012 to achieve this mission.

MHA's long term target for law enforcement and fire-fighting efforts. £1,041 million, which amounts to 63.2% of MHA's budget, will be spent to achieve this desired outcome. The bulk of this amount will be channelled to the operations of SPF and SCDF. The primary functions carried out under SPF include upholding the law, protecting life and property, preventing crime and disorder, detecting and apprehending offenders, and preserving security

47

within mainland Singapore and Singapore Territorial Waters. SCDF's functions include protecting and saving lives and property via the provision of fire fighting, rescue and emergency ambulance services.

A new Marina Bay Fire Station cum Neighbourhood Police Centre will be developed in the Marina South area. The development is essential to enable SPF and SCDF to provide rapid operational response to occupants of the Integrated Resorts, and exhibition and convention centre, tenants of high-rise residential apartments and commercial buildings, and users of the many land and water based leisure attractions being built in the area.

SPF video surveillance systems will be expanded to cover Orchard Road and Central Business District to complement SPF's effort in policing these two strategic locations in Singapore. With the creation of these Public Camera Zones, SPF will be able to perform opportunistic monitoring of the locations covered by the CCTV cameras. The presence of these CCTV cameras will also help to deter crime and provide a valuable source of information in our fight against terrorism.

External CCTV systems will be linked to SPF's Unified Close Circuit Monitoring System. This will involve integrating the CCTV systems of key strategic partners belonging to the Integrated Resorts and the Public Transport System to create a large pool of CCTVs that the SPF can harness for its policing use. By linking strategic CCTV systems that are available in the public and private sectors to a central monitoring centre, SPF will have access to a larger network of CCTV systems from which images can be selected to meet its virtual policing needs.

Land and floating barriers will be extended along the coastline to strengthen the coastline defence against illegal landings. The physical barriers have proven to be very effective in deterring illegal landings and the proposed extension is one of SPF's strategies to strengthen the coastline defence and optimise resources in safeguarding our shores by concentrating resources in strategic locations.

Other areas of expenditure

Efficient registration of groups and people

Registration services provided to people and groups. £87.5 million, constituting 5.3% of MHA's budget, will be spent to achieve the desired outcome. This outcome will be achieved through facilitating the provision of immigration and registration facilities, such as the issuance of travel and identification documents, birth and death registration, processing and granting of immigration passes, Permanent Residence and Citizenship status. MHA will focus on expanding the existing registration capacity and improving the e-services to the public.

Secure borders with efficient and legitimate flow of goods, people and conveyances MHA's critical role in safeguarding borders, while at the same time ensuring an efficient and legitimate flow of goods, people and conveyances through Singapore's borders. £207 million, constituting 12.6% of MHA's budget will be spent to achieve the desired outcome.

This outcome will be achieved through deployment of resources at the checkpoints to conduct stringent border security checks and take enforcement action against illegal immigration and illegal importation of goods. Some initiatives include the provision of people and goods clearance services at the new International Cruise Centre (ICT).

Secure and humane custody of prisoners

The secure and humane custody of offenders in Prisons contributes to the MHA's mission to make Singapore safe and secure. £113 million, which constitutes 6.9% of MHA's budget, will be spent to achieve this desired outcome. Among the initiatives and programmes, £7.5 million will be set aside for the ongoing redevelopment of the Changi Prison Complex (CPC).

The CPC is part of a master plan to centralise prison facilities at a single locality. This centralisation will allow the streamlining of operations and more effective mobilisation of resources in times of emergencies. It also facilitates the return of the lands occupied by various low-density penal facilities to the State, thereby optimising the use of land resources.

Effective rehabilitation of prisoners

MHA recognises that effective enforcement is only one part of the equation. Successful rehabilitation of inmates and reintegration of ex-offenders will steer them towards becoming contributing members of the society and reduce re-offending. £72 million will be spent to achieve this desired outcome and this constitutes 4.4% of MHA's budget.

A society free from drug activities

This desired outcome captures the long term target of our operations in narcotics control. £28 million, constituting 1.8% of MHA's budget, would be spent to achieve this. CNB will continue to intensify its enforcement efforts through regular island-wide operations and intensive raids against drug traffickers and abusers.

CNB will continue to enhance its operational and intelligence capabilities by leveraging on technology and through better management and analysis of strategic intelligence information to complement tactical intelligence on the ground.

A Singapore well-prepared for emergencies, civil disasters and unconventional threats

This desired outcome captures MHA's aim to provide robust Homeland security for Singapore, to prepare Singapore well for effective response during emergencies. £81.5 million, which constitutes 5% of MHA's budget, will be spent to achieve this desired outcome. Among the initiatives and programmes, Civil Defence public shelters will continue to be constructed in MRT stations along the Circle Line (CCL) and Downtown Line (DTL).

Successful partnership with the community to maintain a safe and secure society

To maintain safety and security in an increasingly complex operating environment, the community is a key partner of the Home Team. The community plays an increasingly important role in supporting the work of the Home Team to make Singapore a safe and secure home. £11.5 million will be spent to achieve this desired outcome. This constitutes 0.7% of MHA's budget.

MHA will continue to engage the community via educational institutions, grassroots organisations and self-help groups through public education programmes. Besides the current public education programmes that are targeted at different groups in society, such as students and the working population, MHA continues to think of innovative ways to engage members of public so as to raise their level of emergency preparedness. For example, SCDF will be building an Emergency Preparedness Learning Centre (EPLC) in the Central Fire Station. The EPLC will have interactive simulators and exhibits for visitors to learn more about topics like smoke evacuation, fire safety and tremors in a hands-on manner. The EPLC is targeted to be completed in the early part of 2012.

Known I.T opportunities in Defence and Security

MINDEF have a few key projects aimed at enhancing its operational effectiveness through the development of corporate IT systems. These projects include an improved Healthcare System, which seeks to provide better quality healthcare services to MINDEF and Singapore Armed Forces (SAF) personnel via the streamlining of business process and the integration of military healthcare records with national healthcare systems; as well as an Electronic Balanced Scorecard System, which automates the performance evaluation processes of MINDEF and the SAF units. DSTA outlined its intent to develop new capabilities in the next three years. Two major projects to be implemented in FY 2012 are the transformation of the DSTA Intranet to improve information accessibility as well as promote collaboration and connectivity among its staff. The other project was a new Enterprise Resource Planning (ERP) system that is expected to increase productivity and business efficiency within the organisation. MHA will be procuring AIMSIII, which is a framework agreement which covers the application and infrastructure development, support and maintenance for MHA systems. Among many initiatives from the Home Team departments, the Singapore Police Force intends to acquire systems to enhance road-safety enforcement such as the Digital Traffic Red-Light System and Digital Speed Enforcement Camera System. Separately, the Immigration & Checkpoints Authority (ICA) will be implementing a Flexi Immigration Clearance System which allows the ICA to flexibly toggle between automated and manned counter for immigration clearance. This system allows the ICA to boost operational capabilities.

Chapter 11: Biotech and Pharmaceutical Opportunities in Singapore

Singapore embarked on its Biomedical Sciences (BMS) initiative in 2000 to develop the pharmaceuticals, biotechnology, medical technology and healthcare sectors, as part of its move to a knowledge based economy. Since then, the BMS sector has grown rapidly, and it is now the second-largest manufacturing cluster, with nearly 90% of the output from pharmaceuticals, followed by medical devices.

The manufacturing sector contributes to a quarter of Singapore's economy. Singapore aims to grow its BMS output to £12.5 billion by 2015, which is well on track with ongoing public and private sector investment.

Singapore was rated among the world's top 5 biotech spots by Fiercemonitor, in 2007.

The BMS sector is driven by three key bodies, the Agency for Science, Technology and Research (ASTAR), the Economic Development Board (EDB), and the Ministry of Health (MOH), with high level advisory committees to chart its course. The biomedical city, Biopolis, now in its phase IV, locates public and private R&D centres, while Tuas Pharma Park offers shared facilites for pharmaceutical manufacturers. A medical technology cluster in the west will be developed to accelerate its growth.

There are now 12 global pharmaceutical and biotechnology companies in Singapore who have invested in over 25 commercial manufacturing facilities. Another seven plants are set to open in the next three years. The BMS sector was predicted to grow between 5 - 10% in 2012. Total output stood at £10.5 billion in 2009, accounting for 10% of total manufacturing output.

Over 100 global biomedical sciences companies have leveraged on Singapore's world class manufacturing capabilities, clinical and scientific infrastructure, connectivity to Asian markets and pro-business environment to carry out a range of activities from cutting-edge research and clinical trials, to manufacturing and regional headquarters in Singapore.

R&D

A new national research structure was set up in 2006, with the Research, Innovation and Enterprise Council chaired by the Prime Minister, under the new National Research Foundation.

NRF allocated £2.5 billion over 5 years for 3 targeted sectors:
1. biomedical
2. Sciences
3. Environment and water technologies
4. Interactive

5. Digital media

R&D funds from NRF, ASTAR and the Ministry of Health are primarily channelled to research into areas such as oncology, eye diseases, infectious diseases, and medical devices. Other R&D programmes to spur life sciences research include The Translational Clinical Research programme run by the National Medical Research Council, and the Clinician-Scientist Award, among others.

There are over 4,300 researchers engaged in BMS R&D in 50 companies and 30 public sector institutes, with an annual R&D budget of around £0.5 billion. The government will invest £1.8 billion in BMS research from 2011- 2015, a 12% increase over 2006-2010. The key focus will be better integration of research performers across the BMS landscape; greater emphasis on translational and clinical research (TCR); and stronger focus on economic outcomes.

The BMS Industry Partnership Office (IPO), was set up in 2010 to better integrate research efforts, and as a one stop shop for BMS companies that wish to engage multiple Singapore agencies in research collaborations.

Pharmaceuticals

Leading pharmaceutical companies such as GlaxoSmithKline, Merck Sharp & Dohme, Schering-Plough, Wyeth, Pfizer, Abbott, Novartis, Lonza have set up large scale manufacturing facilities in

Singapore. Fixed asset investments reached £0.6 billion in 2009.

Following large scale investment from API manufacturers, Singapore is now focusing on biologics, and has attracted US$2 billion worth of investments in the last four years, for 6 new plants.

A number of pharmaceutical MNCs also have their Asia Pacific HQ in Singapore. Besides sales, marketing and distribution, they also undertake R&D, and six new R&D bases were established in 2009. They also partner Singapore's multi-disciplinary scientific and clinical network to develop new drugs and therapies resulting in 3 key industry partnerships in 2010.

Biotechnology

Considerable investment has been made to nurture and grow the sector. While BMS Phase 1 focused on basic science and Phase 2 on moving research from the bench to the bedside, phase 3 is aimed at greater integration across agencies, disciplines and the industry to achieve greater economic impact.

The public sector research institutes are increasingly collaborating with universities and hospitals in their translational medicine efforts. The main areas of research are stem cells, oncology, immunology, neurology, metabolic disorders, and infectious diseases. The research institutes are helmed by renowned international scientists and are staffed by skilled local and international scientists.

There is also a growing number of local biotech companies involved in stem cell research, drug discovery and diagnostics.

Medical Technology

There are around 60 medtech companies, mainly MNCs, manufacturing a range of products such as syringes, catheters, hearing aids, contact lenses, stents, pace makers, research instruments and scientific analytical equipment. Several leverage on the scientific and engineering capabilities available in Singapore to develop innovative and cost effective products for the Asian markets.

Singapore accounts for 10% of the world's supply of contact lenses, half of the world's thermal cyclers, and over 50% of the world's micro arrays. The medtech industry manufacturing target is £2.5 billion by 2012. There is also a strong supporting local industry in electronics and precision manufacturing. In a concerted effort to grow the medtech industry, £18 million was allocated for scientists to work with universities and hospitals to develop medical devices such as heart stents, pacemakers, diagnostics for stroke and glaucoma, better catheters etc. £10 million was awarded for research projects in November 2009.

Clinical Trials

The Asian clinical trial market is expected to grow by 20%, and Singapore aims to be the regional centre for clinical trials and drug development.

Major CROs such as Quintiles, Covance, MDS Pharma, PPD, Icon etc are established and expanding in Singapore, to address the growing Asian market. Singapore offers a strategic location in Asia to access a diverse patient base, efficient logistics, Government commitment to the life sciences sector, skilled investigators and manpower, and a good regulatory environment to ensure patient safety during clinical trials.

Singapore was ranked as one of the most competitive countries globally for conducting world class research in a 2006 survey by KPMG, the only Asian country besides Japan.

New Projects

The BMS landscape in Singapore is dynamic and continues to draw in new players while current companies expand their footprint. Some recent developments include:

1. Six new biologics manufacturing facilities at around £1 billion to open from 2011 onwards.
2. New/expansion of pharmaceutical plants.
3. New research labs by pharmaceutical manufacturers and medical devices companies.
4. New regional headquarters by MNCs for the Asia Pacific market.
5. New plants by cardiac products manufacturers.
6. New set ups and expansion by clinical trials companies.

7. New set ups by international companies that supply a range of products, equipment and services to the entire BMS industry.

Chapter 12: Education and Training Opportunities in Singapore

Singapore is a small island city with a population of just over five million. It remains one of the wealthiest countries in the world; according to the International Monetary Fund, Singapore's GDP per capita ranks 3rd globally. In 2010, the Singapore economy was the second-fastest growing in the world.

The Singapore Government places a heavy emphasis on education, training and skills development, as the country's economy shifts from low-cost manufacturing to higher value-added activities (e.g. R&D, financial services, advanced engineering, etc.).

Education took up more than 20% of the 2011 Budget that was announced by the Government in March. This was the second-largest allocation, after defence. Expenditure on education for the fiscal year 2010 was almost £5 billion. In 2010, the Government also announced that it will spend £1.25 billion over the next 5 years to build a comprehensive Continuing Education and Training (CET) system that will help workers develop competence in more complex tasks, mastery of skills and depth of expertise in every trade and profession.

Serious Games

In January 2011, the Media Development Authority of Singapore (www.mda.gov.sg) and the Serious Games Institute of United Kingdom (www.seriousgamesinstitute.co.uk/) announced two initiatives that aim to create opportunities for game companies from Singapore and UK to work together:

(i)   A joint call-for-proposals on serious games.
(ii)   The setting up of a Games Solution Centre in Singapore.

The joint call-for-proposals will allow companies to receive mentorship from the Serious Games Institute in terms of game design and R&D. Under this initiative, MDA will, over two years, commit £2.5 million to fund selected projects.

The Games Solution Centre will enable Singapore game companies to benefit from the established R&D and training capabilities of the Serious Games Institute.

The MDA-SGI partnership will allow UK game companies to hub their activities in Singapore, and use Singapore as a launch pad for their ambitions into the Asia market.

ICT Resources for Schools

One of the master plans for IT in education is to provide access to an IT-enriched school environment for every child. All schools in Singapore already use IT as a resource, giving rise to a constant demand for learning software for all subjects across all educational levels.

Tertiary Education

Degree Programmes: The Singapore Institute of Technology (www.singaporetech.edu.sg/) was established to provide an industry-focused university education in partnership with local polytechnics of which Singapore has five and reputable overseas universities.

SIT is responsible for planning, managing and implementing degree programmes offered by the overseas universities in partnership with the polytechnics. At steady state, SIT plans to offer places to 2,000 full-time students. The duration of SIT degree programmes would typically be about two years for students with the requisite qualifications.

Some programmes offered through SIT by UK Universities are the Bachelor of Engineering with Honours in Naval Architecture by the University of Newcastle and the Bachelor of Science with Honours in Nursing Practice by the University of Manchester.

Institute of Technical Education: The Institute of Technical Education (www.ite.edu.sg) is looking to offer diplomas in hospitality, pastry making, beauty therapy courses which is not offered in the polytechnics.

Private Education Institutions (PEIs): Private Education Institutions, such as the Singapore

Institute of Management (http://www.sim.edu.sg) and the Management Development Institute of Singapore (http://www.mdis.edu.sg/), have tie-ups with foreign universities, though there are still requests for university partnerships.

Some programmes offered through these PEIs by UK Universities are the Bachelor of Science with Honours in Economics by the University of London and the Master of Business Administration by the University of Wales.

Specialised Schools

In recent years, specialised schools such as the Digital Media Academy (www.digitalmediahub.org), the Singapore Sports School (www.sportsschool.edu.sg) and the School of the Arts (www.sota.edu.sg) have been set up. There are also opportunities to work with training providers niche sectors such as tourism and hospitality, media, wealth management, etc.

Continuing Education and Training (CET): The Continuing Education and Training (CET) Masterplan aims to prepare the Singapore workforce and industry for two shifts:

1) The workforce of the future – nearly 20% of Singapore's resident workforce will have at least a diploma qualification by 2020.
2) Emerging and growth industries – to equip Singaporeans with the skills for job opportunities in new growth industries.

Chapter 13: Singapore Political and Economic Overview

Political and Economic

Check out the latest political and economic updates on Singapore Government

Singapore is the region's most politically stable country. Singapore practices a modified version of the Westminster Parliamentary system. Each parliament sits for a maximum of five years.

The last General Election was held on 7 May 2011. The ruling People's Action Party (PAP) has been dominant since 1959, before Singapore became independent and the PAP currently holds 81 of the 87 elected seats in Singapore's single chamber Parliament. The Workers' Party is the largest opposition party in parliament. More details can be read at www.parliament.gov.sg

The elections for President are held every 6 years with the last one held in August 2011. Details on the Singapore President are at www.istana.gov.sg

There are no direct elections for local government. A system of regional Mayors and town councils exists.

International Relations

Singapore is an active player on the international stage. Singapore is a founder member of the Association of South East Asian Nations (ASEAN), the regional grouping comprising Singapore and nine of its immediate neighbours. Singapore participates in the Asia Pacific Economic Cooperation (APEC) forum, Asia-Europe Meeting (ASEM), and is a member of the Commonwealth of Nations and the United Nations. Singapore attended the 2010 G20 summit in South Korea as a leading member of the Global Governance Group (or '3G') which is made up of nations outside of the G20.

Singapore enjoys good relations with its neighbours.

Economic Overview

The Singapore economy weathered the global financial crisis well. Its financial system proved resilient, having emerged consolidated, well-capitalised and conservatively regulated from the 1997/98 Asian financial crisis. It needed neither bank bailouts nor did it experience major disruptions of credit flows. With one of the highest trade-to-GDP ratios in the world, Singapore was however hit by the subsequent economic crisis and the slump in global demand, with export-dependent manufacturing suffering the most.

Singapore was the first Asian country to slide into recession in 2008, hitting bottom with a 0.8% contraction in 2009. It has since witnessed a remarkable V-shaped recovery. This comes at the back of a global rebound in manufacturing as well as strong activities domestically, including the opening of the 2 integrated resorts in early 2010.

It posted its fastest annual GDP growth on record of 14.8% in 2010. Economic growth has eased considerably since with a 4.9% expansion in 2011, on the back of lower manufacturing growth particularly in electronics and biomedical clusters.

Barring any external shocks, the government is forecasting a 1-3% GDP growth for 2012, given the subdued global economic outlook. External-oriented sectors are expected to remain weak, with the electronics sector likely to be particularly hard hit. Inflation (at 5.2% in 2011) continues to be a key challenge but is expected to moderate to between 2.5 to 3.5% in 2012. Labour market remains tight, with the lowest unemployment rate in 14 years, at 2% in 2011. Key long term challenges facing the government are raising productivity growth and reducing heavy reliance on foreign labour. Budget 2012 unveiled in February included key measures aimed at addressing these.

Chapter 14: Business Risk Singapore

Bribery and Corruption

In Singapore there is zero tolerance for bribery. Any attempt to bribe or otherwise prevent an official from carrying out their duties can result in arrest.

In Singapore the Corrupt Practices Investigation Bureau (CPIB) is the government agency which investigates and prosecutes corruption in the public and private sectors. It was established in 1952 by the then British authorities. The CPIB's primary function is to investigate corruption. It is also empowered to investigate other criminal cases in which corruption may be involved.

Incorporated within the Prime Minister's Office, the Bureau is headed by a director who reports directly to the Prime Minister. The CPIB is independent of the Singapore Police Force and other government agencies so as to prevent any undue interference in its investigations. The CPIB is empowered to detain suspects of corrupt practices without trial.

Singapore was ranked 5th (of 183) in Transparency International's Corruption Perceptions Index (CPI) in 2011, after New Zealand, Denmark, Finland and Sweden.

Visit the Business Anti-Corruption portal page providing advice and guidance about corruption in Singapore and some basic effective procedures you can establish to protect your company from them.

Terrorism Threat

There is an underlying threat from terrorism in Singapore. Attacks could be indiscriminate, including in places frequented by expatriates and foreign travellers. The Singapore Government has put in place extensive measures to combat terrorism and has arrested a number of terrorist suspects. They have measures in place on several levels including military, internal security, border, infrastructure security and civil defence. To bolster its preparedness, Singapore participates actively in international counterterrorism efforts.

Violent crime is rare in Singapore. But visitors are advised to be alert at all times particularly of suspicious characters and behaviour; these may be reported to the premises' managers or directly to the Singapore Police Force at phone number 999.

The Singapore Police Force has established the Police MRT Unit on the Mass Rapid Transit network to protect the public transportation system. Personnel from the Special Operations Command and the Gurkha Contingent are also deployed to complement other police officers on patrol. The Police Coast Guard is active inspecting ferries and other vessels in Singapore territorial waters.

All anti-terrorism activities in Singapore are overseen by the ministerial-level National Security Coordination Secretariat.

Intellectual Property

Intellectual Property (IP) rights are territorial, that is they only give protection in the countries where they are granted or registered. If you are thinking about trading internationally, then you should consider registering your IP rights in your export markets.

In Singapore IP is protected by patents, trademarks, registered designs, copyright, and layout-designs of integrated circuits, geographical indications, trade secrets and confidential information, as well as plant variety.

The Intellectual Property Office of Singapore (IPOS) is a statutory board under the Ministry of Law. It was created as the lead government agency that advises on and administers intellectual property (IP) laws, promotes IP awareness and provides the infrastructure to facilitate the development of IP in Singapore.

As Singapore's IP regulator and policy advisor IPOS maintains a robust and pro-business IP regime for the protection and commercial exploitation of IP.

Singapore's Intellectual Property Rights legislative and administrative regime is fully compliant with TRIPS or Trade Related Aspects of Intellectual Property Rights. It is also a signatory to several international conventions on IP protection on patents, copyrights, industrial design among others.

Organised Crime

As with terrorism, the Singapore Government takes a serious view of organised crime and has in place several severe measures to counter it. These measures include the use of the mandatory death penalty against drug and firearms traffickers; jail and fines for those caught for human and goods trafficking; strict rules and expensive entry charges to discourage Singaporeans from patronising the casinos at its two integrated resorts; close monitoring of designated red-light districts.

Visitors from the UK are advised not to become involved with drugs of any kind: possession of even small quantities can lead to imprisonment or the death penalty.

Chapter 15: Conclusion

Given that Singapore is 8 hours ahead of GMT, companies need to maintain effective communications with their customers despite the time differential. This is particularly important given the emphasis that Singaporean place on developing and maintaining relationships.

Singapore is relatively high cost compared to its neighbours and has a tight labour market. Consequently, the government particularly encourages investment in high-tech, automated and capital intensive industries. Most recent investment has been of this nature, concentrating especially on life sciences, advanced engineering and petrochemicals.

Companies whose activities require unskilled or semi-skilled labourers should be aware of the Foreign Workers Levy (payable for each overseas employee) and the quota system which limits the ratio of foreign workers to Singaporeans.

Most labour intensive manufacturing has moved out of Singapore to lower cost markets in the region. By contrast, the Singaporean government actively encourages experts and other professionals, particularly in new technologies, to set up in Singapore.

Singapore is:
1. Ranked number one globally by the World Bank in its "Ease of Doing Business" report.

2. An international financial centre and trading hub for the region, with excellent transport connectivity.
3. An ideal springboard to South East Asia.
4. The fourth largest foreign exchange trading centre in the world.
5. The UK's largest trading partner in South-East Asia and one of its largest export markets outside Europe.

Singapore has a sophisticated financial services sector and most forms of payment are accepted. The most common are:
1. Bank demand draft
2. Telegraphic transfer
3. Letters of credit (sight & term)
4. Open account; and
5. Collection basis

Prices are usually quoted in Singapore dollars.

There is no requirement for local equity participation in businesses established in Singapore, and these can be up to 100% owned by a foreign national or company.

Potential investors should initially seek assistance from the Singapore Economic Development Board (EDB), the statutory board responsible for promoting inward investment. EDB is a one-stop agency which facilitates and supports investors in both manufacturing and services sectors, as they move up the value chain to achieve higher sustainable returns and seek out new business opportunities.

Part 2: CEO Guide to Doing Business in Malaysia

Chapter 16: Introduction

Are you a CEO, consultant, or entrepreneur interested in entering or expanding your activity in the Malaysia market?

Then this book is for you!

The main objective of this book is to provide you with basic knowledge about Malaysia; an overview of its economy, business culture, potential opportunities and an introduction to other relevant issues. Novice exporters, in particular will find this book a useful starting point.

Today, Malaysia is the world's largest producer of computer disk drives and rubber and one of the largest producers of timber. It is the world's largest exporter of palm oil (US$14.58 billion in 2009) although second to Indonesia in terms of production. State-controlled car manufacturer, Proton, which owns the Lotus brand, is expanding on a global scale.

Malaysia is a multi-ethnic society of 28.4 million people, with a majority Muslim population. Sixty-six per cent of the population are Ethnic Malays, approximately 25 per cent Chinese and the remainder is made up of Indians and indigenous people. Around 10 million are under the age of 18.

The country is a federation of 13 states and three federal territories, situated on the South China Seas. It is famed for its beautiful beaches, stunning scenery and dense rainforests. There is a burgeoning tourism industry with considerable room for expansion. Despite the global economic downturn Malaysia remains in a strong economic position. In 2009 the Malaysian Government unveiled a US$16 billion economic stimulus plan and Bank Negara Malaysia, the Malaysian Central Bank, reduced interest rates to 2 per cent (although they have since increased to 2.75 per cent). The country aims to achieve Developed Nation status1 by 2020 and recently published its tenth five-year economic plan outlining how it intends to achieve this.

Decades of strong industrial growth and political stability have made Malaysia one of South-East Asia's most vibrant and successful economies. Strong GDP growth has raised per capita income to US$6,764 (2009) with a forecast GNI in 2012 of US$9,610. This has transformed a commodities-based economy into one with a large, export-orientated manufacturing sector, and an economy with aspirations towards the service sector, particularly with the rise of the Islamic finance industry.

Chapter 17: Malaysia at a Glance

The criteria for becoming a Developed Nation includes high GDP per capita, strong industrialisation and a high Human Development Index rating (combining economic measure with other measures, such as life expectancy and education).

Full name: Federation of Malaysia

Capital: Kuala Lumpur

Administrative capital: Putrajaya

Area: 329,847sq km

Population: 28.4 million

Ethnicities: Ethnic Malays (66 per cent), Chinese (25 per cent), Indians (8 per cent), others (1 per cent)

Major languages: Bahasa Malaysia (official language), English, Chinese dialects, Tamil, Telugu, Malayalam

Life expectancy: 72 years (men), 77 years (women)

Major religions:	Islam, Buddhism, Taoism, Hinduism, Christianity, Sikhism
Labour force:	11,561 million
Unemployment:	364,000 (3.1 per cent)
Monetary unit:	Ringgit Malaysia (MYR)
Stock markets:	Bursa Malaysia (previously known as the Kuala Lumpur Stock Exchange)
Value of exports:	MYR553,295 million
Export commodities:	Electronic equipment, petroleum and liquefied natural gas, chemicals, palm oil, wood and wood products, rubber, textiles
Value of imports:	MYR438,015 million (Jan-Oct 2010)

Value of major import products:

(Jan-Nov 2010) Machinery and transport equipment (MYR239.0 billion or 49.6 per cent of total imports); Manufactured goods and articles (MYR88.5 billion or

18.4 per cent of total imports); Mineral fuels, lubricants, etc (MYR47.6 billion or 9.9 per cent of total imports); Chemicals (MYR44.0 billion or 9.1 per cent of total imports); and Food (MYR27.4 billion or 5.7 per cent of total imports).

Member of:

The Commonwealth, the UN, the Asia-Europe Meeting (ASEM), the Association of Southeast Asian Nations (ASEAN), the Non-Aligned Movement (NAM), Asia-Pacific Economic Co-operation (APEC) and the Organisation of The Islamic Conference (OIC).

A leading choice for investors; Malaysia's strategic position between the Indian Ocean and the South China Sea, coupled with its strong economy and stable political environment, make it a popular choice with investors.

The development of projects such as the Multimedia Super Corridor and Iskandar Malaysia in Johor will only increase the country's investment appeal. Malaysia's key industries are: electronics, petroleum and LPG, chemicals, textiles, palm oil, timber, and tourism.

Traditionally, the UK has been one of the country's leading investors, with estimated cumulative investments of over £20 billion in the last 30 years. As Malaysia opens up its services sector to foreign firms it will create excellent opportunities for UK companies, which have a global reputation in this sector. Both the tourism and car manufacturing sector also have considerable scope for expansion.

Malaysia is an active player on the world stage and a founder member of the Association of Southeast Asian Nations (ASEAN). The country sees itself as a leader in the Islamic and developing world. Malaysia's Prime Minister, Mohd Najib bin Tun Abdul Razak, is a British-trained economist who has pledged radical reforms and more transparent government.

Chapter 18: Malaysia Strong Links with the United Kingdom

There are strong ties between the UK and Malaysia, based on a thriving trade and investment relationship. The UK is Malaysia's largest market in Europe and Malaysia is the UK's second-largest market for goods in South-East Asia, after Singapore. Close historical and educational ties, a familiar commercial and legal framework and the widespread use of English have all cemented this close relationship.

UK exports in 2009 (goods and services) to Malaysia were worth £1.68 billion, the same level as 2008. UK imports from Malaysia over the same period totalled £1.85 billion. In 2009 the value of UK services exports to Malaysia was £634 million.

A substantial and growing number of UK companies have a presence in Malaysia and many use the country as a hub for their regional business interests.

One-third of the 21,000 skilled jobs in Malaysia's Multimedia Super Corridor have been created by British firms. The Malaysian education and training market is worth £240 million a year to the UK. Around 40,000 Malaysians take UK qualifications in their home country and 13,000 travel to the UK each year to study. They include the current Malaysian Prime Minister, who studied at Nottingham University and Malvern College and subsequently encouraged the university to set up a campus in

Malaysia. More than 80 UK institutions have links with Malaysian counterparts.

Defence Bilateral

Defence relations between the two countries are also strong and form an important part of the Five Power Defence Arrangements (FPDA), which also involve Singapore, Australia and New Zealand. Malaysia has made a valuable contribution to UN peacekeeping forces in various countries.

Inward investment

Malaysia's inward investment in the UK is also substantial and growing, with 17 firms listed in London; five on the London Stock Exchange, 11 on AIM and one on the PLUS market. In total, there are more than 50 known investments in the UK. Sports car manufacturer, Lotus, is owned by Proton; YTL owns Wessex Water; and MUI owns iconic UK brands Laura Ashley and the Corus hotel chain. Malaysian companies are also majority shareholders in Crabtree & Evelyn and Costains. One of the world's leading centres for rubber research and development, the Tun Abdul Razak Research Centre, is located in Hertfordshire, while Malaysia's international gaming company, Genting, acquired Stanley Leisure in 2006 for £700 million and also has a 10 per cent stake in the Rank Group.

Chapter 19: Opportunities in Malaysia

We have designated Malaysia as a High Growth Market and identified significant opportunities in the following sectors:

Retail

Tesco and Giant are the leading supermarket retailers in Malaysia. Tesco's revenue in 2009/2010 was approximately £750 million and this is expected to rise as more stores open. Tesco employs over 15,000 people and sources a lot of its products from within Malaysia, so it is a significant contributor to the Malaysian economy.

Oil and gas

Shell has substantial operations and ongoing investments in Malaysia, including a retail business of more than 800 petrol stations (the largest in the country). In total, Shell investments have created almost 6,900 jobs in Malaysia.

Facilities and infrastructure provider Petrofac won the rights to develop an offshore block in conjunction with leading oil and gas corporation, Petronas. The initial investment of around £8 million (MYR56 million) will be supplemented by further plans for investment in the future. In December 2010 Petrofac was also awarded a US$280 million contract to develop an offshore early production system off the east coast of Malaysia.

Malaysia is also fast becoming the regional centre for subsea engineering and procurement activities, with many well-known names like Technip, FMC Technologies, Aker Solutions and others establishing a manufacturing base in the country. Many UK oil and gas service providers and equipment suppliers are doing well in the market, thanks to the UK's strong reputation in Malaysia.

Defence

The Euro fighter consortium is actively promoting the aircraft in Malaysia, given the need for a new-generation multirole fighter that can be effective against many of the other aircraft in the region. Kuala Lumpur has asked for information on the Typhoon, Boeing F/A-18E/F Super Hornet and the Saab Gripen.

Initial aircraft assessments have begun, with Malaysian officials expected to visit Euro fighter facilities in the near future. Funding for an initial payment is likely to be included in the next Malaysian five-year economic plan. The Government of Malaysia decided to construct the Malaysia Defence and Security Technology Park (MDSTP) at Sungkai, Perak; and Blenheim Capital, which provides offset consulting, announced that it had entered into an agreement to support and promote the project.

The MDSTP will be the first of its kind in the ASEAN region, catering to the growing demand and needs of the defence and security industry. Its core purpose is to become a regional defence hub, providing the necessary facilities and infrastructure for research and development, production of equipment and parts, maintenance, repair and overhaul and other technical services related to the defence and security industry.

Education and skills

The Malaysian education and training market is worth over £240 million a year to UK institutions and companies. The rapid development of this sector and growing business opportunities has made Malaysia one of UK Trade & Investment's top four priority markets. It will soon become the "Education Hub" of the ASEAN region and £10 billion will be allocated each year for developing this sector, under the tenth Malaysia Plan (2011-2015) and Economic Transformation Programme. Some of the focus will be on skills training, English language, pre-school education and R&D. The three Ministries involved in developing the sector are the Ministry of Education, Ministry of Higher Education and Ministry of Human Resources.

Nottingham University's branch campus was the first in Malaysia and it celebrated its tenth anniversary in 2010. Newcastle University's Medical School, Marlborough College and Epsom College will be opening campuses in Malaysia by 2012. There are 13,500 Malaysian students in the UK furthering their studies and an additional 40,000 doing British programmes in Malaysia.

Aerospace

Since 1999 BAE Systems has placed work packages worth in excess of MYR1,300 million (nearly £200 million) with various companies in Malaysia. Rolls-Royce has also placed substantial work in Malaysia, including a MYR120 million (£18 million) contract for the supply of high-tech composite components for its V2500 engine. The company has won contracts to supply aero engines to both Air Asia and Malaysia Airlines, and in May 2009 Rolls-Royce announced a £75 million contract to service Ardour engines on the Royal Malaysian Air Force's Hawk fleet.

In addition, UK companies supply legacy work programmes, including parts and components for the older Airbus aircraft (A320s, A330s, A340s and A380s). In 2009 Spirit Aero Systems (the largest independent supplier to Airbus and Boeing) set up a manufacturing base in Malaysia. It is expected to expand further to take work from the new A350 and B787 programmes.

Construction

The Malaysian Government launched the "Green Buildings Mission", which provides funding (approximately MYR1.5 billion) and tax incentives for developing green technology and promoting the construction of green buildings. There be a further development allocation of MYR230 billion for

2011-15 construction opportunities. Malaysia aims to achieve Developed Nation status by 2020. Construction continues to be an essential element of the Malaysian economy and there is an urgent need for green building. The Malaysian "Going Global" initiative will also encourage its contractors to venture into the UK market.

Green technology

The Malaysian Government established a cross-sector incentive for green technologies in 2009. The budget for green technologies is MYR1.5 billion; however, as of August 2010, approved green technology financing was just MYR112,935,000 – less than 8 per cent of the total available budget. Uptake of the fund has been slow due to the lack of clarity concerning what constitutes a "green" technology and the licensing process. As of January 2011 this has been improved. While the value of the incentive is MYR1.5 billion, the potential value of the green technology industry will be substantially more.

The Malaysian Government will cover 2 per cent of the total interest on any loans required by companies and guarantee 60 per cent through the Credit Guarantee Corporation (M) Berhad. The remaining 40 per cent will be covered by the bank/private finance. This is available up to a maximum of MYR50 million for suppliers and MYR10 million for consumers.

Financial and business-related services

Islamic finance in its modern form is approximately 30 years old and is some way from reaching maturity. The sector is currently growing fast and has received a great deal of support from the Malaysian Government which has developed Kuala Lumpur to become the leading centre for Islamic finance in Asia. The Islamic finance sector is also a priority for the City of London. In February 2009 UK Trade and Investment signed a memorandum of understanding (MOU) for co-operation with Malaysia's Central Bank – Bank Negara.

A great deal of activity has flowed from this MOU and we expect this to continue through 2012 and beyond. UK-based Islamic banks have been active in Malaysia and there are opportunities for other firms in the sector, or for those providing services to it such as legal services, transaction services, asset management and education. HSBC, Standard Chartered, Barclays and RBS are all active in Malaysia. HSBC and Standard Chartered, two of the longest-established foreign banks in the country, have opened major back-office processing centres in the Multimedia Super Corridor (MSC) involving substantial investment and new jobs. Prudential Assurance Malaysia Berhad is the largest British insurance company in Asia and one of the largest in Malaysia. Aviva and Friends Provident both have joint ventures with Malaysian partners. Life sciences GlaxoSmithKline (GSK) is Malaysia's leading pharmaceutical and consumer company with a turnover of £120 million. It has a significant manufacturing facility serving regional markets and it employs over 800 people. In September 2009 GSK invested £2 million in a global IT support centre based in Malaysia, employing 130 people. The company plans to invest a further £11 million over the next two years and increase employment to around 400 people.

Creative media

The creative industry contributed around 1.6 per cent of GDP in 2009. The focus for developing the industry is on creative multimedia – especially animation for simulation, advertising and entertainment – and games development. The MSC Malaysia Animation and Creative Content Center (MAC3) Co-Production Fund was established by the Multimedia Development Corporation (MDeC) and helps Malaysian companies collaborate with reputable foreign firms to build skills and technologies.

A Creative Industry Policy will be formulated and the Digital Terrestrial Television Broadcasting (DTTB) project will be rolled out to help spur the expansion of related creative industries. With DTTB technology, more content will be delivered more efficiently.

Software

The use of ICT is being promoted by the Malaysian Government in all industries. MSC Malaysia (formerly known as the Multimedia Super Corridor) is identifying and supporting the development of niche areas in software and e-solutions, creative multimedia, shared services and outsourcing, as well as e-business.

Cloud computing services will be developed to provide SMEs with critical software applications for customer relations management, enterprise resource planning, supply-chain management, human resource management and financial and accounting management. Niche areas for applications development include healthcare, education and financial services (especially in Islamic banking).

Telecommunications

The main telecommunications providers in Malaysia are TM, Maxis, DiGi, Time and U Mobile. Government-linked TM has extensive telecommunications infrastructure for Malaysia's highly urbanised population. In September 2007 the company split its fixed-line and mobile businesses into two separate companies, TM (fixed-line business) and TM International (mobile business).

TM International rebranded itself in May 2009 as Axiata Group, which includes TM's domestic mobile operator, Celcom, as well as international mobile subsidiaries in Asia. The telecommunications sector revenue amounted to MYR35.5 billion in 2009, an increase of 0.08 per cent on 2008. Opportunities for investors include new technologies telecommunication equipment, optical fibres, synthesis equipment, new generation networking and digital equipment.

Chapter 20: Malaysia Geography and Climate

Geography Malaysia is situated in central South-East Asia, bordering Thailand to the north and Singapore and Indonesia to the south. The land area is 328,550sq km. It comprises Peninsula Malaysia and the states of Sabah and Sarawak (East Malaysia) on the north coast of the island of Borneo. The major islands are Langkawi, Penang and Pangkor off the west coast; and Tioman, Redang, Kapas, Perhentian and Rawa off the east coast. Mount Kinabalu, at 4,094 metres, is the highest peak in Malaysia.

Malaysia has an equatorial climate, with uniform temperatures throughout the year. Temperatures range from 32°C during the day to 22°C at night. It is cooler in the hill country. Rainfall is common throughout the year, averaging 200-250cm a year.

Centres of business Kuala Lumpur is the capital and the second largest city of Malaysia, with an estimated population of 1.629 million (2008). Greater Kuala Lumpur, also known as the Klang Valley, is the fastest-growing metropolitan region in the country. The Parliament of Malaysia is located here, as is the King's official residence. Kuala Lumpur is home to the tallest twin buildings in the world, the Petronas Twin Towers.

Putrajaya is the federal administrative centre of Malaysia. It is a planned city, located south of Kuala

Lumpur. The seat of Government was shifted to Putrajaya from Kuala Lumpur in 1999, due to the overcrowding and congestion in the capital. Named after the first Malaysian Prime Minister, Tunku Abdul Rahman Putra, the city is situated within the Multimedia Super Corridor beside Cyberjaya, a planned new township with a science park at its core. The Multimedia Super Corridor (MSC) is a government-designated zone designed to spearhead Malaysia's information and technology growth. The MSC includes an area of approximately 750sq km which stretches from the Petronas Twin Towers to Kuala Lumpur International Airport. The MSC offers attractive tax breaks, high-speed internet connections and proximity to the airport. The Multimedia Development Corporation, MDeC (formerly MDC), was created to oversee development of the MSC. Iskandar, Johor is also known as Iskandar Development Region and South Johor Economic Region. It is a major 2,215sq km development zone, two-and-a-half times bigger than Singapore and 48 times the size of Putrajaya. Its role is to attract investment and business to the region. Iskandar, Johor encompasses Johor Bahru, Johor Bahru Tengah, Kulaijaya, Pasir Gudang and Nusajaya.

Chapter 21: Working with Agents and Distributors in Malaysia

Direct sales into the Malaysian market can be difficult, and for most UK companies it is more effective to approach the market through local business partners (agents and distributors) who have the ability to distribute and provide locally based technical support. Licensing and franchising are also increasingly popular options. It is possible to set up a representative office, a branch office, a joint venture or a wholly foreign-owned enterprise in Malaysia. If you are planning to do business in Malaysia, consult a lawyer about the possible options and how you plan to conduct the business.

An agent is a company's direct representative in a market and is paid commission, whereas a distributor buys products from the manufacturer and sells them on to customers. The difference between the cost of purchasing products and selling them on (the profit) forms the distributor's income. Entering a market by working with an agent or distributor can have several advantages. It reduces time and costs, and companies gain the local knowledge and networks of the agent/distributor. However, employing a third party results in an additional cost to your products and you may also lose some control and visibility over sales and marketing. It also has implications for intellectual property rights protection, increasing the risk of your product being copied or counterfeited. Given these considerations, you need to select agents and distributors carefully.

Suggested questions to ask agents and distributors are listed below. You should also conduct due diligence to verify this information.

1. Company size, history and ownership (private or state-owned) Quality and quantity of the sales force, Customer feedback and trade/bank references
2. Regional coverage: Types of outlets covered and frequency of visits; Transportation and warehousing facilities Are they right for you?
3. Does the agent/distributor have a genuine interest in representing your product? Can they benefit from actively promoting your interests (is it a win-win)? Do they also represent any competing companies/products? Can you communicate effectively with your counterpart?

Once a working relationship has been established, the agent/distributor needs to be managed actively. This may be achieved by the following:

1. Visiting as regularly as is practicable.
2. At a senior management level. This shows interest in and commitment to, the agent and the market. It will also provide you with an opportunity to learn about conditions in the market and see how your products are doing.
3. Working closely with the agent to show them how they can profit from your products.

4. Helping to prepare marketing and sales Plans for the agent.
5. Providing regular training for sales staff and after-sales training for technical staff in the UK.
6. Linking performance to incentives and agreeing milestone targets.

Chapter 22: Malaysia Additional Market Entry Options

Licensing and franchising

A successful business in Malaysia will almost certainly have a Malaysian partner and this is essential to qualify for any Government project funding. Licensing and franchising is one approach to selling products and services, but the exact business model will vary, depending on the sector and company.

Legal structures

A business in Malaysia may be conducted by an individual as a sole proprietor (Malaysian citizen only), by two or more (but not more than 20) persons in partnership, by a locally incorporated company, or by a foreign company registered under the provisions of the Companies Act 1965.

Companies Commission of Malaysia

All sole proprietorships and partnerships must be registered with the Companies Commission of Malaysia (CCM) under the Registration of Businesses Ordinance 1956. In the case of partnerships, partners are both jointly and severally liable for the debts and obligations of the partnership, should its assets be insufficient. The Companies Act 1965 governs all companies in Malaysia. The Act stipulates that a person must register a company with the CCM in order to engage in any business activity. It provides for three types of companies: a company limited by shares, where the personal liability of its members is limited to the par value of their shares and the number of shares taken or agreed to be taken by them. A company limited by guarantee, where the members guarantee to meet liability to an amount nominated in the Memorandum and Articles of Association in the event of the company being wound up. Or an unlimited company, where there is no limit to the members' liability.

Representative offices

Representative offices are often the first step taken by foreign companies when establishing a permanent presence in Malaysia. They provide a vehicle through which the foreign investor can undertake activities such as market research, customer liaison and support. Representative offices can also organise business visits from company headquarters, which can make the process of obtaining business visas for visitors much easier. Public relations work and local administration are also permitted. However, a representative office cannot conduct sales activities. This means they cannot sign contract, receive income or issue invoices and tax receipts. Applications to establish a representative office should be made to the Malaysian Industrial Development Authority (MIDA).

Branch offices

Branch offices can be used for companies that own property in Malaysia but do not plan to have their head office there, and need the ability to exercise their rights based on the Malaysian legal system.

Registration to become a branch office is made with the Companies Commission of Malaysia (CCM). A registration fee is payable, based on the authorised share capital of the parent company. A higher registration fee is payable if the parent company has a high authorised share capital.

Joint ventures

A joint venture (JV) is an organisation jointly owned by one or several Malaysian and foreign partners. A JV can be formed by way of equity contribution, whereby ownership, risk and profit are shared, based on each party's monetary contribution. Alternatively, a JV can be incorporated, with liabilities and profit distribution being decided by contractual agreement. JVs can be beneficial in a number of ways. A good local partner may contribute market knowledge and strong marketing and distribution channels, and they may help reduce the costs and risk of market entry. In Malaysia a local partner is essential for gaining Malaysian Government contracts and, although there is a drive towards liberalisation, the Government still has a considerable stake in many industries, including agriculture and utilities.

The challenge of establishing and running a successful JV is to find and nurture the right partnership. Partners have to overcome issues such as mismatched expectations and differences in business culture and practices. The ability to maintain effective communication, and control where necessary, is also crucial.

It is essential that you carry out corporate and financial due diligence before you sign up to any partnership. Companies should also plan an exit strategy and ensure that any contractual agreements include an appropriate opt-out provision.

Wholly foreign-owned enterprises (WFOE)

A wholly foreign-owned enterprise (WFOE) is a company incorporated in Malaysia that is 100 per cent owned by a foreign organisation/organisations. Where permitted, WFOEs are a popular option for foreign companies, as they give the investor complete control over their business entity, as well as allowing them to enjoy the full profit from its operation. Compared with a joint venture WFOEs also generally give greater protection to the investor's intellectual property rights.

A WFOE allows the foreign investor to issue invoices and receive revenues in MYR. This model is only available in certain sectors of industry, but with further liberalisation of the services sector there should be a relaxation of these arrangements. MIDA has more information on its website www.mida.gov.my. This is a vital first point of reference for UK companies as MIDA has the authority to change/negotiate depending on the type of company and the scale of investment.

Foreign-invested commercial enterprises (FICE)

A foreign-invested commercial enterprise is a type of incorporated business entity. New and existing investors can apply to incorporate a FICE in Malaysia.

Chapter 23: Malaysia Market Entry Due Diligence

Many of the problems that foreign companies encounter when doing business in Malaysia could have been avoided by carrying out some due diligence at the outset.

There are different levels of due diligence, appropriate for different situations. If your sole interest is in exporting, the best proof of a Malaysian company's ability to pay is a letter of credit from the bank. If a company can produce this you do not need to check its financial standing as the bank will have already done this.

A very simple piece of due diligence is to obtain a copy of a company's business licence. This will tell you the following:
1. The legal representative of the company.
2. The name and address of the company
3. The amount of registered capital, which is also its limited liability.
4. The type of company.
5. The business scope.
6. The date the company was established and the period covered by the licence.

You should check that the information contained in the business licence matches what you already know and, if it doesn't, find out why. If you want to verify the information externally, you should go through the

Companies Commission in Malaysia (www.ssm.com.my/en/index.php). You will have more security if you know who the legally responsible person is, so find out who you are dealing with. The shareholders of the company are responsible for that amount of liability as registered capital on the business licence. You can check whether or not the registered capital has been paid up by using a firm of accountants to get a Capital Verification Report.

If you want to establish a business relationship that goes beyond exporting, you will need to carry out further research. It is not enough simply to obtain a copy of a company's accounts, as they may not be accurate. Accounts in Malaysia are unlikely to be audited to the standards routinely expected in the UK, and companies may have different sets of accounts for different audiences, so it is advisable to use such data in conjunction with information obtained from elsewhere. Good-quality consultancy and assistance is available from firms resident in Malaysia and the UK. These companies can carry out operational, financial, legal and technical due diligence checks, typically by looking at the actual operation of the business and building up a more accurate picture by carefully interviewing people who work in and with the firm.

Chapter 24: Employing Staff in Malaysia

Malaysia has a young workforce that is disciplined, educated and trainable. Young people who enter the labour market will have undergone 11 years of school education, up to secondary school level. Workers in Malaysia are generally keen to acquire new skills.

Skills development

To cope with the manufacturing sector's demand for highly skilled workers, the Malaysian Government has taken measures to increase the number of engineers, technicians and other skilled personnel graduating each year from local educational institutions, as well as foreign universities, colleges, technical and industrial training institutions. The Human Resources Development Fund (HRDF) was launched in 1993 and is aimed at encouraging direct private-sector participation in skills development with a grant from the Malaysian Government.

The HRDF operates on the basis of a levy/grant system. Employers who have contributed to the system qualify for training grants for their Malaysian employees. For more information please visit the Ministry of Human Resources in Malaysia website (http://www.mohr.gov.my).The Employment Act 1955 stipulates the minimum conditions of employment for employees in Malaysia.

Recruitment channels

There are several channels for recruiting staff in Malaysia:

1. Job online services such as www.bestjobs.com.my/ and www.mycen.com.my/malaysia/job.html.
2. Classified adverts for jobs in English are available in English daily newspapers such as the Business Times, New Straits Times and The Star.
3. Trade journals for key industry sectors, such as the Malaysian Timber Bulletin and Water21.

Carry out due diligence. This includes conducting personal background checks and checking all references before offering them the position. Offer appropriate remuneration. Details on remuneration and the minimum conditions of employment can be found on the Malaysian Industrial Development Authority (MIDA) website.

Overseas training

Offering employees the opportunity to train overseas is also very attractive at all levels. Make sure that, in return for providing such training, employees make a commitment to stay with your company for a specified period of time. A lot of smaller companies setting up an office in Malaysia may well just employ one person to deal with all aspects of running the company. Although this may be convenient and cost-effective, it might not be the best way to run your operation.

If your employee is not familiar with the rules and regulations pertaining to running an international office or business in Malaysia, then you may soon have to deal with issues of non-compliance, which could prove very costly. Moreover, having one person in control of all financial and legal aspects of the business is obviously risky.

Working hours

Working hours in Malaysia are 9am to 5pm, Monday to Friday 9am to 1pm, Saturday Government offices tend to work:8.30am to 4.30pm All public service departments and some banks close on the first and third Saturday of the month.

Public holidays

The most important festivals of each religious group in Malaysia are designated as public holidays. Muslim festivals are timed according to local sightings of various phases of the moon and the dates given are approximate. During the lunar month of Ramadan that precedes Hari Raya Puasa, Muslims fast during the day and feast at night and normal business patterns may be interrupted. Buddhist festivals are also timed according to phases of the moon, so variations may occur.

Interpreters may be required for business meetings, particularly outside major cities, and for the avoidance of doubt; all important negotiations should be carried out with an interpreter present. It is also advisable to have all written documents translated into Malaysian, as your business counterparts in Malaysia will not necessarily indicate if they do not understand something however, English is widely spoken and is the language of international business. Ethnic groups speak a variety of languages and dialects.

Chapter 25: Marketing in Malaysia

To reflect the fast-moving nature of the Malaysian marketplace, which is continuing to liberalise at pace, your marketing strategy will need to be continually reassessed and refined. Sales literature, Trade shows and exhibitions are a good way of meeting potential new customers, but you still need to persuade them to buy your product. Sales literature needs to be effective in English and, if possible, in Bahasa Malaysia and you need to decide what kind of advertising is appropriate.

Product and service adaptations

You may need to adapt your product or service to meet the needs of the Malaysian market. Marketing research can help you to identify any adaptations you need to make.

Brands Retailing tends to be quite different from the UK, particularly for premium brands, which are not sold through own-brand outlets. For example, in Malaysia a premium pair of sunglasses would only be sold through optical outlets/opticians.

Brand is very important and, although home brand strength is improving in areas such as generic health and hygiene products (for example, soaps and shampoos), consumers still prefer to purchase products that are supported by brand names and guarantees.

Sales promotion

Companies that appoint local partners can usually be guided by them with regard to the type of advertising and sales promotion that would suit the launch of their product/s.

The media

Malaysia has some of the toughest censorship laws in the world, although the internet is unregulated and the main outlet for political debate. The authorities regard foreign influences as potentially harmful and are keen to protect the largely Muslim population from these influences, particularly via television.

News is subject to censorship and entertainment and music videos are likely to have scenes featuring kissing and swearing removed. These laws can have a significant impact on advertising and marketing activities, and foreign companies are strongly advised to talk to UKTI representatives in Malaysia who can put them in touch with local marketing specialists that are accustomed to working within the country's strict controls.

TV and radio: TV3 is the leading national, private terrestrial broadcaster. State-owned Radio Television Malaysia (RTM) operates two television networks and many of the country's radio stations. Private stations broadcast in Bahasa Malaysia, Tamil, Chinese and English.

Newspapers: Newspapers are required to renew their publication licences annually and publishing permits may be subject to suspension or revocation. The news agency for Malaysia is state-run Bernama.

Internet: According to Internet World Stats, 16.9 million Malaysians were online in June 2009. The Government uses domestic laws to censor internet content but has stopped short of introducing filters at Malaysia's internet gateways.

Once you have made contact with a Malaysian company, it is likely that your day-to-day phone and email communication will be in English, with one of the company's English-speaking members of staff. If the standard of English in the Malaysian company is not satisfactory, it is advisable to ask for parallel texts in Bahasa Malaysia and get them translated to ensure proper understanding. If you are going to sign anything as obvious as it sounds; make sure you get it translated first by an independent translator.

Do not rely on your supplier's translation and do not be pressurised into signing anything that you do not fully understand. Most breakdowns in overseas business relations occur because of fractured communications and mutual misunderstandings. If Malaysia is likely to become a significant part of your business you may wish to consider hiring a Malaysian-speaking member of staff. You might also consider taking up the challenge of learning Bahasa Malaysia yourself. However, even if you do achieve a level of fluency, an interpreter or Malaysian-speaking member of staff is still essential for business meetings.

Chapter 26: Business Issues and Considerations

The Malaysian market is a magnet for foreign direct investment. However, while the country's familiar commercial and legal framework and widespread use of spoken English makes it a popular choice among UK investors, there are some significant cultural differences and challenges to be aware of.

While English is generally considered the language of business in Malaysia you may need to employ interpreters during formal meetings and negotiations to prevent any misunderstandings.

There are two forms of interpreting.
1. Consecutive interpreting means you speak and then your interpreter speaks; this is the usual form for meetings, discussions and negotiations.
2. Simultaneous interpreting involves the immediate translation of your words as you speak them. This requires special equipment and can be expensive. It is generally used only for large seminars and conferences.

Interpreting is a skill requiring professional training. Just because someone is fluent in English and Bahasa Malaysia, it does not necessarily mean that they will make a good interpreter. If you are giving a speech or presentation remember that the need to interpret everything will cut your speaking time approximately in half (unless using simultaneous interpreting). It is essential to make sure that the interpreter can cope with any technical or specialist terms in the presentation. If you are giving a speech give the interpreter the text well in advance and forewarn them of any changes.

To get the best out of your interpreter, hire a well-briefed professional interpreter. Though this is likely to be expensive, it will be money well spent. Have your own interpreter available, even if your Malaysian counterparts have one for their side. With your own interpreter you should also be able to get some post-meeting feedback concerning the nuances of what was said (and just as importantly not said).Try to involve your interpreter at every stage of your pre-meeting arrangements. The quality of interpretation will improve greatly if you provide adequate briefing on the subject matter. Ensure your interpreter understands what you are trying to achieve. Speak clearly and evenly with regular breaks for interpretation.

Do not speak for several paragraphs without pause. Your interpreter will find it hard to remember everything you have said, let alone interpret all your points. Conversely, don't speak in short phrases and unfinished sentences. Your interpreter may find it impossible to translate the meaning if you have left a sentence hanging.

Avoid jargon, unless you know your interpreter is familiar with the terminology. Listen to how your interpreter interprets what you have just said. If you have given a lengthy explanation but the interpreter translates it into only a few words, it may be that they have not fully understood. Or they may be wary of passing on a message that is too blunt and will not be well received by the audience. Make sure that your message is getting through clearly and is delivered in a tone that will not cause resentment.

Management Control and Quality Assurance

UK companies use a variety of management control and quality assurance techniques in Malaysia. These include extensive travelling by UK personnel, a controlling or liaison presence in Malaysia and providing extensive training and management for Malaysian staff. It is important not to allow milestones to slip by, whether these are attending a board meeting in a joint venture or arranging a quality audit at a supplier's. Particular attention to detail should be paid when sourcing products from Malaysia. Specifications can be easily misunderstood, so they need to be very clearly explained and agreed, and a quality management system put in place with the Malaysian company. Consultancies can undertake all or part of this process on your behalf.

Bribery and Corruption

Corruption remains an issue in Malaysia. Anyone doing business in the country is likely to encounter, or hear of, corruption in one form or another. Practices such as facilitation payments, bribes and giving and receiving expensive gifts in order to develop business relationships are still a problem in certain places. Our advice to companies encountering corruption is simple; don't get involved. Not only are there issues of business integrity to bear in mind, but of course it is also illegal. Invariably, corruption is related to lack of professionalism and control, all of which are damaging to long-term business.

Companies should ensure that all of their commercial activities in Malaysia are compliant with the UK Bribery Act. The Malaysian Government has pledged to tackle corruption and streamline bureaucracy as part of its tenth five-year plan, which outlines how it aims to achieve Developed Nation status by 2020.

Chapter 27: Business Etiquette

In a highly competitive business environment it is more important than ever to understand the business culture of your target markets. Understanding business culture helps you to understand, anticipate and respond to unexpected behaviour. It also ensures that you behave in an acceptable way and avoid misunderstandings.

Meetings

In meetings, your approach should be formal but friendly. The most senior person in the team should enter the room first and greet the most senior Malaysian representative. In general, you should introduce older people to younger people and women to men. Make sure that you show due respect and use people's titles correctly.

Malaysians may occasionally look downwards rather than look you in the eye when meeting you, as this is considered a mark of respect. Hierarchy is important when doing business in Malaysia. Leaders should sit opposite one another around the table and, sometimes, Malaysian staff will be seated in descending order of seniority.

Malaysian people like to spend time getting to know their business partners, so don't be surprised if little is achieved in the first meeting, beyond building rapport. Many Malaysians take a keen interest in the

English Premier League and this can be a good icebreaker.

Handshakes

Traditional Malaysian people may be uncomfortable shaking hands with a member of the opposite sex. Foreign men should wait for a Malaysian woman to extend her hand and foreign women should wait for a Malaysian man to extend his hand. In general, it is best to follow the lead of your host, who will dictate the level of formality considered appropriate.

Attire

Malaysians tend to dress appropriately for their work surroundings, as you would expect in the UK. Although suits are common, meetings are just as often held with open collars. Site visits rarely require suits and at evening meetings and receptions it is common to see a mix of traditional batik shirts (colourful silk or cotton long-sleeve shirts that are worn un-tucked from the trousers) and office attire. Women generally cover their chest, shoulders and the tops of their arms.

Hierarchy

Hierarchy is an important concept in Malaysian business. See Meetings (above) for details of how you should conduct business meetings with due regard for people's experience and seniority.

Names and titles

In business, you should use people's professional titles (professor, doctor, engineer) and honorific titles. Malaysian men may use "bin" (meaning son of) and women may use "binti" (daughter of) followed by their father's name. The most common title used for a senior official or businessperson is either "Tan Sri", "Datuk", "Dato" or "Datin" (for women). Datuk is the same term used to address grandparents in Malaysia and is a term of respectful endearment, given to recognise an individual's contribution to society or industry. Where business associates use this as a prefix, you can drop their full name when making introductions, eg "Good morning Datuk". The title "Dato" is awarded by a royal head of state and "Datuk" is awarded by a government official.

Women in business

There are no special considerations, but generally contact is kept to a minimum. Businesswomen in Malaysia will conform to the same types of formalities as men.

Punctuality

You should be punctual for meetings and leave plenty of time for your journey to avoid arriving late. Your hosts may well be late, though, and expect certain reasons to arise frequently, especially the weather and traffic; one usually having a severe impact on the other!

Business cards

Business cards should be exchanged after the initial introductions have been made. Use both hands or the right hand only to exchange business cards. Be sure to treat someone's business card with respect as to do otherwise risks insulting them. Examine the card before putting it away and never write on someone's card in their presence unless they are happy for you to do so. One good tip is to ask a question based on the information on the card. Although these guidelines apply in general, Malaysia is a rapidly modernising and liberal country so it is best to let your host decide.

Negotiations

Malaysians like to spend time getting to know their business associates, so don't expect important decisions to be reached in the initial meeting. Avoid becoming visibly frustrated or irritated as this could insult your host. Malaysian people will pause before responding to a question to indicate that they have given it the appropriate thought and consideration. They regard the Western preference for responding immediately to a question as ill-mannered.

Body language

Non-verbal communication is important in Malaysia. The concept of saving face means that many Malaysians will be indirect in what they say and will avoid a flat refusal. Similarly, when they say "yes" it may purely indicate that they have understood what you are saying, rather than confirming that they wish to proceed. Look for clues in the tone of voice and body language of your host.

Call to prayer

Malaysia is recognised as a Muslim state although there are also large numbers of Hindus, Buddhists and Christians. In Muslim areas the call to prayer from mosques happens five times a day, for several minutes each time. If you are in the vicinity of a local mosque be sensitive to this important religious observation.

Muslims will lower their voice or stop talking completely during the call to prayer.

Gift giving

Giving small gifts, especially of food and crafts, is commonplace in Malaysia and welcomed, but modest presents are best to avoid embarrassing your host. It is worth making a personal touch to the gift to show that it is from either your town/city or company; the thought rather than the worth will be appreciated, especially if it is linked to their favourite English Premier League football team! There are some important factors to consider when giving gifts to particular ethnic groups. For Malays – avoid giving alcohol, non-Halal food or anything made of pigskin. Do not wrap the gift in white wrapping paper (denotes mourning) or yellow wrapping paper (reserved for royalty). For Chinese Malaysians – avoid giving flowers; stick to fruit, sweets or cake. Wrap your gift in happy colours (red, pink or yellow) and give gifts in even numbers as odd numbers are considered unlucky. Avoid white, black or blue. Don't be surprised if your host initially refuses the gift; this is customary to signify lack of greed. For Indian Malaysians, offer gifts with the right hand, or both hands if the gift is large. Use red, yellow or green wrapping paper, but avoid white or black. It is best to avoid alcohol and do not give leather products to a Hindu.

Cultural considerations

There are a number of key cultural differences between Malaysia and the UK that you should bear in mind when conducting business there. Concept of "face": The concept of "face" is important in Malaysia, as it is in many parts of South-East Asia, and Malaysians strive for harmony in their business and personal relationships. To prevent loss of face, Malaysians will avoid confrontation or will tell others what they want to hear rather than tackling issues head-on. For example, rather than say "no" they might say "I'll try." This allows both the person making the request and the person turning it down to save face and maintain harmony in the relationship. Some Westerners can find this approach confusing. Try rephrasing the question in different ways so you can compare the answers you get.

Family

The family is at the heart of Malaysian society and Malaysian people place great value on unity, loyalty and respect for one's elders. Families are relied on for emotional and financial support.

Chapter 28: Regulations, Incentives and Tax

Commercial invoices

For Malaysia, the invoice is combined with a Certificate of Value and Origin (C/VO) which has to be manually signed (facsimile signatures are not accepted).

Special certificates

Whisky imports require a Certificate of Age (minimum three years), as issued by HM Revenue & Customs. Information on regulations and standards for goods imported into Malaysia is published on the Royal Malaysian Customs Department website.

Investment rules and incentives

The Government of Malaysia encourages investments by providing various incentives to investors. Around 300 of the foreign companies in Malaysia are members of the British Malaysian Chamber of Commerce, a bilateral trade organisation based in Kuala Lumpur. The Chamber has corporate members involved in a wide range of industry sectors, including: engineering, construction, automotive, oil and gas, energy, telecoms, IT, education, training, retail, hospitality, publishing, financial services, banking, insurance and corporate services.

Exchange controls

Under exchange control rules travellers may import or export up to MYR1,000 per person into or out of Malaysia without prior approval. There are no limits on the amount of foreign currency (notes and/or travellers cheques) travellers may import. Non-residents may export foreign currency up to the amount they previously imported, provided they have documentary evidence of the amount they imported. All travellers must complete a travellers declaration form on entering Malaysia. Exchange control is administered by the Central Bank on behalf of the Malaysian Government. Most of the authority for payment approval is delegated to authorised banks.

Restrictions

Most goods, with the exception of certain items, may be imported under an Open General Licence. Other licensing requirements need to be met, depending on the type of product or service. However, this can be quite an onerous task and may involve many different licensing bodies.

There are currently 15 Free Industrial Zones (FIZ) in Malaysia, covering ports such as Port of Tanjung Pelepas, Johor, Johor Port, and Port Klang Free Zones. These ports are involved in both industrial and commercial activities. In addition, there are 13 Free Commercial Zones (FCZ) which comprise mostly ports and airports, with the exception of Port Klang Free Zone (PKFZ) which operates as a Free Commercial and Industrial Zone. FCZ with retailing activities are normally situated on the border of Singapore and Thailand and only allow retail trading. Further information on trade facilitation can be obtained from the Royal Customs and Excise Department website in Malaysia.

Customs and tax

Please refer to the Royal Customs and Excise Department in Malaysia for information on customs and tax.

Getting your goods to Malaysia

Malaysia has extensive and modern infrastructure, including major port and airport facilities. There are ports serving Kuala Lumpur at Klang, as well as large ports serving Johor, Penang, Kuching and Kota Kinabalu. There are many other smaller ports serving other cities and towns. The new Kuala Lumpur International Airport (KLIA) serves Kuala Lumpur, with other international airports and cargo centres serving the cities of Johor Bahru, Penang, Kuching and Kota Kinabalu.

Freight forwarding

Sea and air freight services to Malaysia are provided by a range of companies, including TNT, Crown Freight and DHL as well as many local firms. Freight forwarding companies like these can provide advice on the best way to ship goods to Malaysia. It takes approximately three to four weeks to ship goods from the UK to Malaysia by sea, but this will depend upon the level of service and the company providing it.

Courier

There are many companies providing courier services to Malaysia. The main Malaysian postal service provider is Pos Malaysia Berhad. The company was formed from the government-owned Malaysian Postal Services Department or Jabatan Perkhidmatan Pos Malaysia. It provides postal and related services and transport logistics, as well as a range of counter collection and payment agency services. The company holds an exclusive concession to provide mail services through its network of over 850 branches and mini post offices in Malaysia

Chapter 29: Financial and Life Science in Malaysia

Malaysia is one of the Asian countries with plans to become the region's biotech hub. It will leverage on the strength of the country's diverse natural resources. The key strengths of Malaysia include its infrastructure, its existing history and advances in medical devices and diagnostics manufacturing, well regulated pharmaceutical industry, availability of GMP certified manufacturing facilities.

Given Malaysia's traditional focus on agriculture, a large percentage of agricultural biotechnology companies are in adding value to food and crops. The healthcare biotechnology development policy is to contribute towards the advancement of healthcare by exploiting Malaysia's biodiversity for new drug candidates and providing cost effective outsourcing services for biodrug development.

Under the 10th Malaysia Plan (2010-2015), a number of initiatives have been taken to promote regional development and accelerate growth in designated geographic areas. Five growth corridors were identified. The corridors are established to develop certain subsectors of biotechnology. Malaysia will capitalise on the country's biodiversity for commercialising the discovery of health related natural products and bio-generic drugs.

Terms of payment

The method of conducting business in Malaysia is similar to that in the UK, with no special requirements. Payment against invoice is the usual method though payment can be slow at times. It is advisable for UK companies trading with a Malaysian partner for the first time to accept payment by a secure method, such as a letter of credit. Once a relationship has been established, other, less secure methods of payment can be considered.

Banking

Opening hours: Banks in Malaysia are open between 9.30am to 4.00pm, Monday to Friday. Some banks open on Saturdays, but for local transactions only. The central bank of Malaysia is Bank Negara.

Insurance

The private sector in the UK provides credit insurance for exports of consumer products, raw materials and other similar goods. Speak to your banker or insurance broker for more information, or contact the British Insurance Brokers' Association for impartial advice. British Insurance Brokers' Association Tel: +44 (0)870 950 1790 (consumer helpline) Email:enquiries@biba.org.ukWebsite: www.biba.org.uk Private-sector insurance has some limitations, particularly for sales of capital goods, major services and construction projects that require longer credit packages or that are in riskier markets. The Export Credits Guarantee Department (ECGD), a separate UK Government department that reports to the Secretary of State for Business, Innovation and Skills, provides a range of products for exporters of such goods and services. Export Credits Guarantee Department Tel: +44 (0)20 7512 7000 Email:help@ecgd.gsi.gov.uk Website: www.ecgd.gov.uk

Chapter 30: Overseas Business Risk - Malaysia

Information on key security and political risks which UK businesses may face when operating in Malaysia

Political and Economic

Check out the latest political and economic updates on Malaysia

Since 2008 Malaysia has been governed by a coalition which suffered its worst ever electoral performance (though it still has almost a two thirds majority in parliament). The ruling Barisan Nasional (BN) coalition, which has run the country since independence 54 years ago, suffered serious reverses at the March 2008 General Election. Although they still hold 140 of the 222 parliamentary seats, they lost their 2/3rds majority - a significant blow psychologically and operationally (they are no longer able to make changes to the constitution without a parliamentary debate). At state level, the opposition now controls 4 states, which generate about 60% of the economy. The next elections are due by May 2013 although there is speculation that elections will be called by early 2012.

The BN coalition is made up of parties representing Malay, Chinese, Indian and native ethnic interests. The non-Malay parties in particular were seriously weakened in March 08 and are struggling to reform.

There is also significant infighting in UMNO (by far the biggest party in the coalition and the main Malay grouping), primarily the future of the bumiputera law (Article 153 of the Constitution) which provides affirmative action for members of the Malay ethnic group.

The law establishes quotas for educational institutions, public scholarships and government jobs. All companies listed on the Stock Exchange are required to have a minimum 30% bumiputera equity. The aim of the policy is to ensure that the ethnic Malays maintain a controlling interest in the country and aims for an overall 30% share of the country's corporate equity. (Contrast with Singapore, which was expelled from the Malay Federation due to its objections to the imposition of the bumiputera laws and is now primarily controlled by ethnic Chinese).

Prime Minister Najib Tun Razak, who took office in 2009 has focussed on economic development. In 2010 he announced the Economic Transformation Programme aimed at promoting Malaysia to a high income economy by 2020. The programme identifies 12 National Key Economic Activities for development and contains plans for large infrastructure programmes funded by public and private investments. Although Najib is seen a reformist by inclination he faces the loss of his core support if he attempts to withdraw support from the Malay majority.

Following the March 2008 General Election a credible opposition coalition (Pakatan Rakyat - PR)

138

emerged. It is led by Anwar Ibrahim, a former Deputy Prime Minister. The opposition itself is a coalition of ethnic groupings and, in this aspect, mirrors the BN. Similarly it has suffered from internal dissent and has lost much of the momentum gained following the election. However the opposition, sensing an imminent election, have mobilised support on the streets of Kuala Lumpur, ostensibly demonstrating for electoral reform. Denied an outlet through the traditional media (which is controlled by the government) the opposition mounted its 2008 campaign using new media and street rallies. It seems likely that the opposition is gearing up for a similar campaign over the coming months. Although the government is likely to declare many of these rallies illegal and attempt to suppress them there has been none of the violent disorder associated with opposition movements in the Middle East or Thailand.

Since the Asian financial crisis, Malaysia has made good progress in reforming its banking and financial system. Local banks have been consolidated and there is phased liberalisation to allow greater competition. Malaysia has developed its Islamic Finance capability and is now a major hub in the Asia Pacific region. The Government has also progressively dismantled the exchange and other controls imposed during the Asia Crisis - including abandoning the Ringgit peg to the dollar in July 2005 in favour of a managed float.

The chief economic reform challenges facing Malaysia now are to improve the performance of Government Linked Companies (which still account for a large part of the economy); to achieve further progress in corporate governance and transparency, and to move up the value chain in response to the economic challenge posed by China and other low-cost manufacturing economies. The administration has made some changes to improve financial and political accountability, and is seeking to improve Malaysian competitiveness in sectors such as biotechnology.

Bribery is illegal. It is an offence for British nationals or someone who is ordinarily resident in the UK, a body incorporated in the UK or a Scottish partnership, to bribe anywhere in the world.

In addition, a commercial organisation carrying on a business in the UK can be liable for the conduct of a person who is neither a UK national or resident in the UK or a body incorporated or formed in the UK. In this case it does not matter whether the acts or omissions which form part of the offence take place in the UK or elsewhere.

The ruling coalition, the Barisan Nasional (BN), and in particular the largest component party, United Malays National Organisation (UMNO) is regularly confronted by charges of corruption from the opposition. (The recent demonstration in Kuala Lumpur was organised by the "Bersih" movement - "bersih" is Bahasa for "clean"). These have been comprised of allegations of "money politics" to secure positions within the party to charges of distribution of government contracts to cronies and political allies.

Many major companies in Malaysia are GLCs (Government Linked Companies). These are companies in which the government maintains equity holdings and are often the preferred vehicle for implementing government projects, albeit with foreign partners. This has resulted in accusations of anti-competitiveness from some quarters and allegations that revenue is used to fund political activities. The PM has recently addressed these allegations by announcing a programme of closer private sector collaboration and a divestment of assets.

Najib's predecessor as Prime Minister, Abdullah Badawi, embarked on his tenure with a drive to improve the standing of his party by launching a "National Integrity Plan" in 2004. The plan consisted of 5 key objectives:
1. To reduce corruption and the abuse of power.
2. To increase the efficiency of public service delivery.
3. To enhance corporate governance.
4. To strengthen the family.
5. To improve citizens' quality of life.

The Malaysian Anti-Corruption Commission (MACC) was formed on 1st January 2009 modelled on Hong Kong's Independent Commission Against Corruption and replacing the previous Anti-Corruption Agency. The Commission has launched a number high profile investigations since its formation.

Malaysia was ranked 56 (of 180) in Transparency International's corruption perception index in 2010.

The country is a signatory to the UN Convention against Corruption, the UN Convention against Transnational Organised Crime and the ABD-OECD Plan for Asia-Pacific. It was named on an OECD blacklist of uncooperative tax havens at the 2009 G20 summit but has since been removed following agreement to implement OECD recommendations.

Visit the Business Anti-Corruption portal page providing advice and guidance about corruption in Malaysia and some basic effective procedures you can establish to protect your company from them.

Terrorism Threat

There is a generalised threat in Malaysia from both terrorism and kidnapping. Terrorist threats come predominantly from the al-Qa'ida-linked Islamist group Jemaah Islamiyah (JI) who remain active in Malaysia, as well as from other groups such as the Abu Sayyaf Group (ASG) who are based in the southern Philippines but operational in Malaysia. Although the Malaysian government has been effective in reducing the terrorist threat posed by JI, the threat from indiscriminate terrorist attack remains. There is also potential for spill over from the insurgency in southern Thailand to spill over the border into Malaysia.

In particular, there is a general threat from kidnapping by both terrorist and criminal groups. The threat is higher in Borneo than in peninsular Malaysia. JI regards the peninsula as an area for recruitment and fundraising as opposed to Borneo which has served as a facilitation centre and location for kidnappings. ASG also kidnaps for ransom, but its targets to date have been predominantly locals rather than expatriates.

Intellectual property protection

Intellectual property protection in Malaysia comprises that of patents, trademarks, industrial designs, copyrights, geographical indications and layout designs of integrated circuits. Malaysia is a member of the World Intellectual Property Organisation (WIPO) and a signatory to the Paris Convention and Berne Convention which govern these intellectual property rights.

In addition, Malaysia is also a signatory to the Agreement on Trade Related Aspects of Intellectual Property Rights (TRIPS) signed under the auspices of the World Trade Organisation (WTO). Therefore, Malaysia's intellectual property laws are in conformance with international standards and provide adequate protection to both local and foreign investors, although there can be problems with enforcement (as in many countries).

Organised Crime

The size of indigenous crime syndicates are limited although trans-national crime networks are active in the fields of counterfeiting goods and credit cards, human trafficking, prostitution and smuggling. Piracy has effectively been eradicated in the Straits of Melaka since the establishment of the Malaysian Maritime

Enforcement Agency in 2004 although there are indications that small scale activities are beginning to return, particularly off the coast of Sabah.

There is evidence of growing human trafficking into and through the country particularly in Sabah from the Philippines. Illegal immigrants frequently end up working as indentured labour or as prostitutes. The State Department's 2010 Trafficking in Persons Report places Malaysia on the Tier 2 Watchlist. Security at the borders has been tightened by the introduction of biometric controls at entry points and the deployment of army patrols along borders. Improvements in both the numbers of personnel and the assets of the MMEA have strongly reinforced the country's maritime borders.

The government is working hard to improve both its physical and technological capabilities in order to address a growth in transnational crime. The numbers of police on the streets in urban areas has grown visibly over the past year and the number of reported criminal incidents has fallen markedly in line with key performance indicators set by the PM. The government is reaching out to other nations to cooperatively tackle trans-border crime. Cybersecurity is a key issue for the government.

Chapter 31: Retail Opportunities in Malaysia

Malaysia national pastime is shopping!

Malaysia has affluent and growing middle-class with a desire for high quality foreign goods. 60% of population is in the middle to high income group with growing purchasing power.

Trade

1. UK and Malaysia ties remain strong based upon a thriving trade and investment relationship (£3.52bn bilateral trade goods and services 2009), close historical and educational ties, a familiar commercial and legal framework and the widespread use of English.
2. Malaysia is the UK's 35th largest export market for goods (2nd in South-East Asia after Singapore), worth £1.2billion in 2010 (+18%).
3. Ranked 21st globally by the World Bank for 'ease of doing businesses.'

The outlook for retailing is positive with the country's improved economy and rising consumer confidence. The retail sector contributed about £12bn (RM57bn) to GNI in 2009 and created almost 500,000 jobs.

1. With rising living standards, consumer buying habits have changed from the simple need for

sustenance to sophistication. Lifestyle fashion, health and beauty have risen in consumer importance, resulting in a demand for designer brands.

2. With rising living standards, consumer buying habits have changed from the simple need for sustenance to sophistication. Lifestyle fashion, health and beauty have risen in consumer importance, resulting in a demand for designer brands.

3. Malaysia has a young population with 32% aged 15 years and below and 63.5% in the 15-64 years age group.

4. The peak sales period takes place during July/August each year, timed with the arrival of tourists from the Middle East.

5. Expansion plans in Malaysia's shopping malls offer many opportunities to international players, where there is already a strong British presence. Current malls regularly refurbish and reposition themselves, while new, large malls are coming up and expanding in the suburban areas to offer Malaysian wider access to popular brands.

High Food and Beverage Spending in Malaysia

1. With a young population of 28.3 million, Malaysia is one of Southeast Asia's most developed nations with per capita income of US$7,700. 61% of the citizens are belonging to the middle-to-upper-income group.

2. Food and beverage expenditure accounts for 25% of the total consumer spending. The per

capita food and beverage consumption in Malaysia is forecast to reach a regionally impressive US$479 in 2012.

UK & International retail brands present in Malaysia

Marks & Spencer, Clarks, Body Shop, Royal Doulton, Hugo Boss, Warehouse, Debenhams, Tesco, Jardines, Dr Martens, Top-shop, Tiffany & Co, Massimo Dutti, Armani Exchange, Mikimoto, Liz Claiborne, Coach, Ralph Lauren Children, United Colours of Benetton, Thomas Pink, Anya Hindmarch, Ted Baker, DKNY, Paul Smith, Mulberry, Paris Hilton, Tommy Hilfiger and Zara.

Malaysia has a dynamic mass grocery retail sector with international retailers like Carrefour, Dairy Farm, Jusco and Tesco. Expansion plans have been confirmed by the retail majors regardless of the impact of the downturn in economic growth. Value sales of food and beverage products through modern retail outlets are forecast to increase by 36.9% by 2013.

Tesco has 39 hypermarkets and supermarkets throughout Malaysia with new outlets planned.

Chapter 32: Security Opportunities in Malaysia

Malaysia is a thoroughfare through which nationals of other South-East Asian countries are transported, mostly to Australia but also to Europe.

Smuggling is a concern, both in and out of Malaysia. The most common contraband is commodities like cigarettes, rice, alcohol and Illegal drugs.

Urban crime reduction is one of the government's key performance indicators, aiming for a 50% reduction by 2015.

Malaysia is considered to be a secure country and there are no serious terrorist incidents on record. There are occasional public order disturbances, mainly political, but these have been managed without incident. The Royal Malaysian Police have however transferred responsibility for CT operations from the Special Branch to a new unit, the Special Task Force.

There is however a number of extra-territorial threats that country faces. Piracy in the Malacca Straits has all but been eradicated thanks to the formation of the Malaysian Maritime Enforcement Agency. (The MMEA was formed, about 8 years ago and has rapidly acquired maritime, air and surveillance assets. They are currently extending their capabilities to the 200nms EEZ boundary).

There remain some concerns over the activities of groups base in other countries, (nominally terrorist but effectively criminal) operating in East Malaysian waters.

Malaysia is a major manufacturing centre for synthetic drugs, such as crystal methamphetamine, which is manufactured in factories based in deep jungle. There are some small arms smuggling, although it is believed that these make their way to criminal, rather than terrorist, hands.

There is widespread evidence of illegal trafficking of persons through Malaysia across its border with Thailand and the government are anxious to restrict the trade.

Malaysia is a thoroughfare through which nationals of other South-East Asian countries are transported, mostly to Australia but also to Europe. The authorities are conscious that traffic is frequently facilitated by corruption.

There are a number of organised international crime syndicates working in the country although the police have, over the past few years, made major inroads into their activities.

Petty crime is rife. Bag snatching is the most common offence. The Prime Minister has made urban crime reduction one of his government's key performance indicators, aiming for a 50% reduction by 2015. The use of CCTV figures centrally in the Home Affairs Ministry's plans to achieve this.

Examples of major projects Infrastructure
1. CCTV surveillance programme for KL and other major city centres.
2. Police communications system upgrade.

Maritime security
1. Ongoing equipping of the Malaysian Maritime Enforcement Agency.
2. Off -shore platform security.

Requirements are not generally advertised but emerge from direct enquiries about capability; through third party agents; through local companies directly appointed; from cold calling.

All security programmes require a local prime. These will often have little or no expertise and add little value.

Business etiquette in Malaysia does not vary much from the UK. English is widely spoken particularly in major cities. Many Malaysians are engaged in international business and are very westernised due to their overseas education or experience working abroad. Frankness, openess and punctuality are all valued traits in business negotiations and dealings.

However the business community in Malaysia reflects the cultural diversity of the country itself. It is important to be aware that each of the three main ethnic groups (Malay, Chinese and Indian) are religiously and culturally distinct and should be approached accordingly.

Chapter 33: Education, Skills and Training Opportunities in Malaysia

Global investors have pin-pointed Malaysia as one of the top markets; within ASEAN, Malaysia is the EU's second largest trading partner, with more than 2,000 EU companies present in Malaysia.

It is fast becoming an 'Educational Hub' of SE Asia and is one of the four priority markets for British products and services related to education and training worth over £250 million a year.

The sector has long been key in the UK-Malaysia relationship. Currently, about 13,500 Malaysian students are in UK to further their studies and an additional 45,000 are either studying for UK degree programmes or undertaking UK professional qualifications in Malaysia. University of Nottingham Malaysia Campus is now in its 11th year. Newcastle University's Medical School, University of Southampton's Engineering School, Epsom College and Marlborough College will be opening by 2012. A number of other British universities and schools are also considering opening their branches here.

Around 60 UK tertiary institutions have links or collaborative arrangements with Malaysian counterparts. These attract students from SE Asia, China, the Middle East and Africa. Currently, there are about 85,000 foreign students and the Government's target is to hit 150,000 by 2015.

Malaysia is fast becoming an 'Educational Hub' of SE Asia... Great importance is being laid on achieving higher standards and improved quality in education and skills."

The Tenth Malaysia Plan and Economic Transformation Programme launched in January 2011, reaffirms the New Economic Model and outlines more measures to transform Malaysia into a high-income economy. This, among others, requires training, re-training and up-skilling of the workforce. Great importance is being laid on achieving higher standards and improved quality in education and skills to face global challenges.

Malaysia's rapid development, political and social stability, close historical and educational ties, a familiar legal and financial framework and the widespread use of English make this an attractive place for British companies to do business. Plus, strategic location from which to penetrate other ASEAN markets, and further into India and China.

The 4th Asia-Europe Meeting for Ministers of Education (ASEMME) will be in Malaysia in 2013 to enhance international cooperation in engaging business and industry in education.

The three ministries related to education and training are the Ministry of Education, the Ministry of Higher Education and the Ministry of Human Resources.

The sector is at the top of the Malaysian Government's agenda for the 10th Malaysia Plan (2011-2015) and was strongly emphasised in the Economic Report with largest sum of £8 billion for the 2011 budget. Thus, opportunities are growing and key areas are detailed below.

Over the next five years, there will be more childcare centres, pre-schools, international and private schools, community colleges, skills/corporate training institutions and foreign branch campuses. Many of the university colleges and polytechnics are being upgraded and given full university status. More institutions are being encouraged by the Government to be involved in R&D and innovation activities, and to work closely with industries. All these will create demand for educational products and services, and business collaboration.

Four educational hubs are being developed, which includes Iskandar Malaysia's 'Edu City' and Kuala Lumpur Education City (KLEC).

Formal Education Structure

The education and training system includes both public and private providers at all levels. It is highly competitive and almost entirely examination orientated. They are now considering revising the examination system. A new comprehensive assessment system, which gives more emphasis to continuous evaluation and creativity to nurture a culture of innovation is being implemented through a pilot project covering 50 schools.

Children have limited allowance to be creative in the classroom and the Government wants to change this and allow greater flexibility in teaching and learning methodology, and in the use of educational technology.

Early Childhood Care and Pre-School Education

Pre-school education is part of the national education system. Children generally begin their education at pre-schools/kindergartens from the age of four to six. The main government agencies that offer this education are the Ministry of Education, the Ministry of Rural and Regional Development (KEMAS), ABIM, the State Religious Department and the National Unity Department.

There is strong focus now on developing Early Childhood Care (Permata scheme) and Pre-school Education under the new Prime Minister - Datuk Seri Najib Razak. Pre-school education will be part of the mainstream public school education system by 2012. Over £20 million has been allocated for this and there are plans to increase childcare centres and pre-schools, and improve teaching and learning in these places. Within the next two years, 87% of children are expected to attend pre-school.

Many of the teachers in the 20,000+ childcare centres and pre-schools are being encouraged to pursue programmes to upgrade from Diploma to Degree and Masters levels. There are calls for joint awarding of qualifications, programme/product development and staff exchange with foreign institutions. As part of this search, the National Association of Early Childhood Care and Education Malaysia (NAECCEM) had a week-long study visit to the UK in November 2010 to look at British expertise, products, services and qualifications available for the sector. Private childcare and pre-school business, especially in the urban areas, are fast growing.

Chapter 34: Construction Opportunities in Malaysia

The construction industry constitutes an important element of the Malaysian economy. Its strength and capability to host of economic sectors and supports to the social development of the country through the provision of basic infrastructure. Although it accounted for only 3% of the GDP in 2010, the industry is critical to national wealth creation. It acts as a catalyst for and has multiplier effects to the economy and also enables other industries namely manufacturing, professional services, financial services, education. The construction industry also provides job opportunities for approximately 800,000 people, with over 68,000 registered contractors in the industry.

Malaysian Construction Industry's gearing up towards Global Competitiveness; with RM230bil allocation for high impact projects through private investments."

The overall building construction market will be further elevated by the 10th Malaysia Plan (2011-2015). The Malaysian government announced that RM230bil has been allocated for development, whereby 60% of it is for infrastructure. The government will intensify the Public-Private Partnership (PPP) and several PPP projects identified under the 10MP will be implemented in 2011 through private investment. Some of the projects are in more involvement from the private sector and investors to engage in public projects, such as construction and management of schools, hospitals and other community infrastructure.

High impact projects identified for implementations are as follows;

1. Develop of Kuala Lumpur International Financial District (Valued at RM26 Bil)
2. Mass Rapid Transit (MRT) system (largest infrastructure project estimate investment of RM36 Bil
3. Mixed development comprising residential, commercial, industrial and infrastructure facilities at the Malaysian Rubber Board's land (valued at RM10 Bil
4. The 100 storey skyscraper, 'Warisan Merdeka' will be the tallest and biggest tower in Malaysia valued at RM5bil targeted for completion in 2015.

Additionally, the Review of the 10MP states that the development of the 5 regional growth corridors in Malaysia. There are Iskandar Malaysia; Northern Corridor of Economic Growth; East Coast Economic Region; Sabah Development Region and Sarawak Corridor of Renewable Energy will incorporate the issues of environment and sustainable development.

In Malaysia, the awareness of sustainability issues in construction and the built environment is increasing. The Malaysian Government launched the 'Green Buildings Mission Campaign' with key government funding of approximately RM1.5bn and tax incentive have been allocated for developing green technology and promoting the construction for 2011-2015

Construction continues to be an essential element of the Malaysian economy, top 10 priorities for urgent needs for Green Building. Malaysia initiative of 'Going Global' will also encourage contractors to venture into the UK Market.

Therefore there are huge potential opportunities within the construction industry in Malaysia for UK companies who wish to develop or expand their business in the region. Particularly, there are opportunities for British expertise, supplies and collaborative initiatives in the areas of infrastructure, environmentally-friendly and intelligent construction.

Malaysian embarked on strategies to achieve "developed nation" status that emphasises skills and technical training and human capital development initiatives in the sector by 2020.

Many projects in Malaysia have successfully used British contractors and consultants. Examples are the KL International Airport, KLCC Twin Towers, Petronas University, power plants, oil & gas and petrochemicals plants, electrified twin tracking railway and urban light rail transport system, to name a few. Successful British firms that have operated in the market include Balfour Beatty, Mott MacDonald, Hyder, Atkins, Arup, Turner & Townsend, Halcrow, Scott Wilson, EC Harris, James R. Knowles, Tilbury Douglas, Bovis, Berkeley Consulting and Powergen.

Chapter 35: Malaysia Economic Overview

Malaysia's economy has been growing steadily, with real GDP growth averaging around 8% prior to the Asian Financial Crisis (AFC, between 1990-1997) and around 5% over the last 10 years. Since the AFC, the country's macroeconomic fundamentals have strengthened considerably. The current account remains in a position of surplus for the 14th consecutive year while the stock of foreign reserves has exceeded USD100bn (around 44% of GDP compared to China's 52%). Banks are well-capitalised, following significant consolidation of banks post AFC and tightening of risk management practices in the banking sector.

As a result, the country was in a better position to handle the global economic crisis in 2009. Despite its high trade openness (exports as a % of GDP ranked 6 the in the world in 2009), the economy was able to rebound quickly from a short recession in 2009 to record a growth of 7.2% in 2010 (2009: -1.7%). The impact of the global crisis was further shortlived owing to accelerated government fiscal stimulus measures (10% of GDP) and aggressive lowering of interest rates.

Consolidation in government finances is progressing very gradually, with the budget deficit reducing marginally to 5.4% in 2011 from 5.6% in 2010: 5.6%. Government debt is mostly ringgit-denominated, but at 53% of GDP is nearing the national debt limit of 55%. Continued rationalisation of subsidies will improve the government's financial position and its capacity to implement reform measures aimed at strengthening the country's economic resilience.

The Malaysian economy is balanced and well-diversified. From a low-income, rural and agricultural country in the 1960s, Malaysia has since developed into an upper-middle-income, manufacturing and services-based economy. The services sector is the largest contributor to real GDP (contributing around 57% of real GDP in 2010) and the largest source of employment (54% share of employment). The manufacturing sector also accounts for a substantial share of real GDP (around 28% for 2010). Electrical and electronic products, petroleum products and chemical products form the bulk of manufactured goods.

Despite agriculture and mining accounting for a smaller share of real GDP (15%), the country's natural resources in crude petroleum, natural gas, palm oil and rubber provide significant cushion to the economy, especially during periods of weakness in the manufacturing sector. Malaysia is still a net oil exporter with total oil and gas reserves of 20.6 billion barrels of oil equivalent in 2009, representing a production life of about 22 years for oil and 41 years for gas. Elsewhere, Malaysia is the world's second largest palm oil producer and exporter (contributing to 45% of world demand in 2009).

Demand in the economy is domestically driven and is largely supported by resilient private consumption on the back of favourable demographics of a young population (50% of the population are below 25 years of age) and a strong labour market (the unemployment rate has averaged 3.4% over the last 5 years). Private expenditure is expected to account for 64.2% of real GDP in 2010, followed by public expenditure at 24.8% of real GDP and net exports at 10-13% of real GDP.

New drivers were introduced in 2010 to spur private investment growth. In 2010, the government under PM Najib, launched a series of growth plans, programmes and reform strategies (New Economic Model, 10th Malaysia Plan, Economic Transformation Programme) aimed at positioning the country for a new phase of growth in order to break out of its middle income status by 2020. The overarching aim is simply to create more high-skilled job opportunities and elevate income levels through value-added economic activities. As such, in place of the old export-led growth model, the government is now focusing on reshaping the business environment in order to encourage the private sector (both domestic and foreign) into investing in infrastructure and development projects all across Malaysia.

There remain however, structural challenges to private investment growth. Malaysia's affirmative policies of the last 40 years have hampered the development of fair competition across business and higher education, causing many educated Malaysians seeking a more level playing field to emigrate abroad.

In addition, the government's persistent fiscal deficit position limits its flexibility to improve Malaysia's infrastructure as well as tax competitiveness compared to regional peers such as Hong Kong and Singapore. The lack of skilled labour, and resulting low value-added in the manufacturing sector as well as relatively high tax rates have all had negative repercussions on private investment growth.

Private investments have fallen to about 10-12% of real GDP and have remained stagnant at these levels over the last 10 years, lower than pre-Asian crisis levels of about 23% of real GDP between 1990-1997. Although, foreign direct investment (FDI) inflows into Malaysia are on the mend after a large decline in 2009, Malaysia's share of global FDI inflows and share of FDI inflows into developing economies arc declining. Unless the government is able to push ahead with marked-out institutional reforms, Malaysia may continue to lose out in private investments to other fast-growing and competitive emerging markets such as China, India and Indonesia.

The continued promotion of competition through liberalisation and deregulation will remain a challenge for the government. The ability to strike a balance between maintaining political stability and pursuing longer-term economic objectives will be a key determinant in Malaysia's growth story over the next decade.

ASEAN forms the core priority of Malaysia's current foreign policy. Meanwhile, Malaysia adopts a watchful approach towards G20 discussions, being aware that decisions may have implications for other non-member countries.

Malaysia's relationship with the IMF has been improving in recent years, after the IMF conceded that it made policy mistakes during the Asian Crisis when it castigated authorities for imposing capital controls. There is now an increased readiness and willingness from Malaysia to increase co-operation with the IMF, with Malaysia agreeing to participate in the IMF's Financial Stability Assessment at the 2010 Article IV Consultation.

Malaysia's interaction in the multilateral arena on international financial institutional reforms will likely be subdued in the near future as the government turns to focus on boosting domestic economic growth and development. Nonetheless, although quiet on the multilateral front, Malaysia continues to move in tandem with IFI reforms and is quietly preparing to adopt BASEL III by the implementation deadline.

Elsewhere, Malaysia continues to be an active participant at WTO discussions and has expressed concern over the slow progress of DDA negotiations. Malaysia was commended by WTO Director-General Pascal Lamy for making clear advances towards greater economic liberalisation. The country continues to display increasing openness towards free trade, judging from efforts to conclude (or at least start on) bilateral Free Trade Agreements with India (concluded in 2011), Australia (nearing conclusion),

USA (through the TPP) and the EU (in progress) amongst others.

Chapter 36: Conclusion

Malaysia is a highly open and diversified economy, with domestically driven demand. Economic activity is spread across services, manufacturing, agriculture and mining sectors.

New and ambitious growth plans take effect this year, aiming to promote Malaysia to developed country status by 2020. Reforms to investment climate and institutional bottlenecks are vital.

Malaysia remains an active participant in WTO discussions and continues to move in tandem with G20 led financial regulation reforms. Malaysia's international economic policies are largely in line with the UK's. Malaysia continues to actively champion free trade and has FTAs with Australia, USA (through the TPP) and the EU in the pipeline.

The UK seeks to boost trade and investment gains with Malaysia, encourage Malaysian "buy-in" into multilateral action aimed at maintaining global economic and financial stability, and support sustainable development of a low carbon economy.

Population: 28.25mn (2010)

GDP: US$238bn (2010) – 37th in the world

GDP per capita: US$8,423 (2010) – 65th in the world

Ease of Doing Business ranking: 18 of 183 (2012)

Corruption Perceptions Index: 56 of 178 (2010)

Human Development Index: 61 of 187 (2011)

Sources: World Bank, IMF, UN

Malaysia has five international airports, and Malaysia Airlines and AirAsia X (budget airline) run frequent direct flights between the UK and Malaysia. Many other airlines also service the route, either directly or via connecting flights. Getting to and from the airport Kuala Lumpur International Airport (KLIA) is located at Sepang, 65km south of the capital. The journey from the airport to Kuala Lumpur city centre is approximately 60 minutes, depending on traffic. Taxis (budget or deluxe) can be obtained from the taxi information desks inside the airport, close to the exit. The fare from KLIA to Kuala Lumpur City Centre is approximately MYR75 (£15) for a budget taxi and MYR100-MYR150 (£20-£30) for a deluxe taxi. An express rail system, the KLIA Ekspres, links the centre of Kuala Lumpur to the airport. The high-speed railway operates at 15-minute intervals. The journey time is 26 minutes. A single journey costs MYR35 (£7) and a return journey costs MYR70 (£14). Travelling within Malaysia Domestic air travel is relatively cheap, with frequent departures to all major cities in Peninsular and East Malaysia (Sabah and Sarawak) through Malaysia Airlines and AirAsia.

The country also has an extensive network of motorways and there are frequent coach departures for travel between cities by road. It is easy to hire and drive a car on a UK licence, though it is perhaps better to rely on taxis in Kuala Lumpur. Taxis are metered and do not expect to be tipped. It can be difficult to find taxis during rush hours or when it is raining.

Below are the essential facts that companies doing business with Malaysia

Need to know

Decades of industrial growth and political stability have made Malaysia
1. One of South-East Asia's most vibrant and successful economies. In 2009 Malaysia's GDP was US$192.8 billion (source: Economist Intelligence Unit).
2. Despite the global economic slowdown, Malaysia's economy remains strong
3. Due to two economic stimulus packages worth £12 billion and a reduction in interest rates (currently 2.75 per cent).The UK is Malaysia's largest market in Europe. Malaysia has made substantial investments in the UK including Lotus, Stanley Leisure, Wessex Water, Star Energy, the Corus hotel chain and Laura Ashley.The UK is a leading investor in Malaysia, with estimated investments of more than £20 billion over the last 30 years.
4. Malaysia is opening up its service sector to foreign firms, and UK companies stand to benefit, thanks to their expertise in the sector.
5. Malaysia has an affluent and growing middle class. The appetite for high quality foreign

goods is reflected in the number of British stores present in the country.

6. Malaysia has made good progress in reforming its banking and financial system.
7. A new wave of liberalisation was announced in May 2009.Malaysia's tourist market is growing rapidly.
8. Malaysia is aiming to achieve Developed Nation status by 2020.

While it is reasonable to expect international business to be conducted mainly in English, your hosts will appreciate it if you use their language whenever possible.

Some common phrases

Good morning:	Selamat Pagi
Good afternoon:	Selamat tengah hari
Good evening:	Selamat petang
Good night:	Selamat malam
Goodbye:	Selamat tinggal
See you again:	Jumpa lagi
Yes:	Ya (as in German yes)
No:	Tidak
Thank you:	Terima kasih
Please sit down:	Sila duduk
Please come in:	Sila masuk
Please:	Sila
Excuse me:	Sila beri jalan (or sila beri laluan)
I come from:	Saya datang dari…
My name is:	Nama saya ialah…
What is your name?	Siapa nama anda?

Part 3: CEO Guide to Doing Business in Indonesia

Chapter 37: Introduction

Are you a CEO, consultant, or entrepreneur interested in entering or expanding your activity in the Indonesia market?

Then this book is for you!

The main objective of this book is to provide you with basic knowledge about Indonesia; an overview of its economy, business culture, potential opportunities and an introduction to other relevant issues. Novice exporters, in particular will find this book a useful starting point.

Indonesia is not the easiest place in the world in which to do business. The 'World Competitiveness Scoreboard' currently ranks Indonesia at 45, only two places ahead of Russia (47), and in stark contrast to countries such as Australia (13), Singapore (2) and the US (1). Clearly, in terms of the measures used by the producers of this scoreboard, Indonesia at the moment is found severely wanting, with its potent brew of traditional cultures, bureaucracy, legal uncertainty and social instability combining to give it the appearance of being a rather hostile place for trade and business. Indonesia is currently undergoing a radical transition towards becoming a more modern and efficient economy, and the road ahead remains uncertain.

Nonetheless, given a proper understanding of cultural, social and legal-regulatory environments, business and investment in most parts of Indonesia is relatively safe and profitable. Many promising changes are underway in Indonesia - notwithstanding the pain being experienced by many sections of Indonesian society; and there is good reason to be hopeful Indonesia shall emerge from its present trial-by-fire to become both an attractive investment destination, and a profitable market for Western products.

This **essay** seeks to give an overview of those elements that are important when undertaking business in Indonesia, including the social and cultural landscape, recent developments regards 'governance', law and legal certainty, business structures, and labour issues. Much emphasis is given to the issue of culture, more specifically, the perceptions, outlooks and/or beliefs that affect human interaction. In the past, perhaps, Western business peoples understanding of 'culture' has been relegated to the realm of manners or etiquette, of simplistic 'do's and don'ts'. However, cultural misunderstanding or miscommunication is generally far more likely to occur at the level of perception and outlook, rather than etiquette. This is not to suggest that etiquette is unimportant, but merely to attempt to shift emphasis from those external or visible cultural expressions to those expressions that are not immediately obvious, in particular as this affects communication.

The Western businessperson in Indonesia must try to remain conscious of the possibility of 'difference' when interacting with Indonesians. Of all the nations of East Asia, Indonesia arguably remains the most

176

strongly traditional in terms of its cultural characteristics and outlooks. In the bustle of Jakarta's traffic, tall buildings and gleaming shopping centres it is all too easy to think of Indonesia as a modern nation, albeit poor, with outlooks and aspirations that more-or-less match those of the West. However, beneath these thin modernist veneers beats the sound of a number of 'different drummers'. Even apparently 'Westernised' Indonesians, including those with a solid Western tertiary education, cannot break free from those patterns, values, attitudes and outlooks formed out of the substratum of their indigenous culture.

Westerners often forget that they too are products of culture. Although far fewer Westerners than in the past profess Christianity, nevertheless Judeo-Christian and protestant humanist values and attitudes permeate the very essence of Western culture. Many Westerners may subconsciously consider these values to be universal in nature, standing above and perhaps even subordinating traditionalist values and outlooks. But whatever our convictions, when communicating with those who may not share a similar worldview, the possibility must be left open that what we believe to be self-evident and/or right may not be shared by everyone.

Chapter 38: Indonesia Political, Cultural, and Geographical Overview

Java sits at the centre of the Indonesian nation. Without Java, there could not be an Indonesia. The 'Javanese' ethnic group occupies the majority of the island of Java. Other major ethno-linguistic groups in Java include Sundanese (West Java), Betawi (from the area around Jakarta) and Madurese. Although Java represents only 7% of Indonesia's total landmass, ethnic Javanese comprise about 45% of Indonesia's total population. Javanese attitudes and worldviews totally permeate the Indonesian bureaucracy, government and military, hence the great importance of understanding the Javanese perspective when referring to Indonesia.

The great majority of Javanese could be said to be very sympathetic to mystical dimensions of human existence. The typical Javanese worldview is based on the essential unity of all existence, in which life itself is a kind of 'religious' experience existing in harmony with a universal order. This worldview emphasises inner tranquillity, harmony and stability, acceptance, the subordination of the individual to society, and the subordination of society to the universe. Inter-personal relations are carefully regulated by customs and etiquette to preserve this ordered state.

These, of course, are the high ideals of Javanese culture that may not always be realised in actual life, as contemporary events in Java frequently demonstrate. In every culture, there is often a distance between ideal behaviour and realty. Nevertheless, the concept of harmony in the Javanese community is a core concept, notwithstanding outbursts of uncontrolled emotion that may occasionally be displayed.

Javanese society and culture is by no means singular or homogenous; it is a complex amalgam of differing tendencies and apparently opposing worldviews. This must be kept in mind when attempting to generalise about 'Javanese culture'; it is not unitary, but rather comprises a composite of influences, both modern and traditional, religious and secular/nationalist.

Javanese society has long been analysed in terms of three major social polarities or worldviews; the abangan (the 'commoners'), the priyayi (the 'nobility'), and the santri (the Islamists, more appropriately referred to as muslimin). These somewhat arbitrary categories should not be interpreted to mean 'classes', but rather as 'outlooks'; ways of looking at and making sense of the world. It is very common in Java to find people of all these outlooks living together under the same roof, and of course, there are very many shades of grey; eg a muslimah may well sometimes adopt haughty priyayi attitudes when socialising with her neighbours, may well believe that manusia harimau (tiger people) inhabit her village, but at the same time be completely devout in her Islamic practice and belief. Although the abangan-priyayi-santri schema is much criticised by academics, mainly because of its tendency to stereotype groups and individuals, its general relevance remains to this day, as the outcome of the 1999 elections clearly showed.

Chapter 39: Examples of Major Projects in Indonesia

Ports

Tanjung Priok is Indonesia's largest international port and needs to expand its facilities to meet growing demand. Four new terminals are planned, with construction of the first scheduled to start at the end of this year and to be completed by 2013. The estimated budget for construction of the first terminal is US$560 million.

The project will be led by Indonesia's port management company, PT Pelindo, and will be offered on a PPP basis. The other three terminals are due to be completed by 2017. There are opportunities for UK companies to design, construct and operate (on a JV basis) the terminals themselves. Despite this planned expansion, Tanjung Priok is expected to be operating at full capacity by 2020 and there are tentative plans for the development of an additional port to manage additional capacity. Airports A US$109 million expansion and renovation of Ngurah Rai International Airport in Bali is expected to begin later this year and to be completed in 2013.

If UK companies secure contracts related to this expansion they will be very well positioned to win business related to the construction of a brand new international airport (runway, taxi ways, apron and parking areas, lighting, airport approach aids, access roads, cargo facilities, cargo apron, hanger) on the north coast of Bali. The cost of the project, which is likely to be offered on a PPP basis, is currently estimated at around US$510m and it's expected to be implemented between 2013 and 2015. The feasibility study for the expansion of Terminal 3 at Jakarta's Soekarno Hatta Airport has just been completed. We await details of the opportunities this expansion will offer.

Prisons

Prisons in Indonesia are currently over-capacity by around 75%. There is a potential lack of security equipment and a programme to procure the requisite products such scanners, protective vets and small arms is being developed. The President has announced a budget for the construction of up to 20 new prisons of around 1 trillion Rupiah (£75 million). However, this may not be sufficient to construct all 20 prisons so the budget being reviewed and a tender to be announced in 2011/12.

Re-equipping emergency services

Possible renewal of Fire fighting and other emergency services.

Maritime Security

The Coast Guard is overseen by the Directorate of Sea and Coast Guard under the Directorate General of Sea Transportation (DGST), and their principle concern is with regard to border protection and protection of shipping. Although it does have a responsibility for Search and Rescue (SAR) there is a separate entity which operates wholly in this area, Badan SAR Nasional (BASARNAS).

Previously part of DGST, BASARNAS now reports directly to the President. It is currently looking to update fleet/equipment and capacity building with particular emphasis on rapid deployment equipment, helicopters, communications and infrastructure.

In 2012 the procurement budget is expected to rise to allow for the expansion of their marine fleet including RHIBs, inflatables, hovercraft, inshore, coastal and ocean-going vessels.

Border Control

The physical geography of Indonesia presents a different problem to that of the United Kingdom – it is an archipelago which consists of 6,000 inhabited islands among its 17,500 islands and its Exclusive Economic Zone (EEZ) comprises the entirety of its internal waters. Policing of these seas and waterways is therefore a priority.

The Palm Oil industry

Valued at £5bn ($7.7bn) for Indonesia it's the country's third biggest export earner. It has brought with it the problem of illegal logging when clearing forest for plantations. The logs are then sold on to gain extra income as part of the plantation process.

As well as the problem of illegal logging and the transportation of the logs via water there are also problems with marine crime (piracy), smuggling, illegal immigration and illegal fishing.

All this represents real potential for UK companies with the skills, expertise and equipment to combat this, in particular providers of surveillance and communications equipment.

Others Courts / forensics

There is a growing recognition for the need to convict based on forensics which could provide opportunities for specialist suppliers.

Hotels

There is a continuing hotel boom in Bali and Lombok is also set for expansion in the hotel trade with a new international airport under construction which should be open in the latter part of 2010 by Angkasa Pura I (State owned airport authority for eastern Indonesia). The major hotel chains have apparently already snapped up beachside real estate in expectation of the tourist boom. Security is a major concern for 4 and 5 star hotels in Jakarta that want to attract corporate contracts, and thus opportunities exist.

The demand seems to follow a recognised trend in the security industry, demand booms after an event and thereafter wanes as complacency sets in. Security was stepped up after the hotel bombings in 2009 and the market is there for CCTV, metal detectors, arches and x-ray machines. However, bearing in mind strong regional and local competition for the low-tech security systems, the feeling among those in hotel security and the supply chain is that UK products cannot compete in terms of price and therefore must find a niche where quality and sophistication are the competing factor. This further diminishes opportunities as there are not many hotels in Jakarta, and less so in other areas of Indonesia, which have the ability and the will to invest the necessary amounts to purchase these systems.

Oil and Gas / Mining

In 2001, Pertamina's monopoly position in the upstream and downstream sectors was removed following the issuance of Indonesia's Oil and Gas Law 22/2001. The company remains a state owned enterprise in an open market where many foreign companies have set up, such as Talisman, BP, Shell, Premier Oil and many others.

While the award of sub-contracts by these companies is overseen by the state regulators BPMIGAS (upstream) and BPH MIGAS (downstream) which are part of the Ministry of Energy and Mineral Resources, there is a strong requirement for security solutions in line with global corporate policy. In effect this means that there is the will and ability to purchase high grade systems for the protection of physical and virtual assets from wells and refineries to office space. However, this should be tempered by the fact that price will always be a major part in any tender process and single tender action is rare and scrutinised by the regulators.

Opportunities also exist in new build facilities and renewal of systems and service contracts in existing operations, specifically in the areas of access control, biometrics, CCTV systems, surveillance, and physical and data protection.

Chapter 40: Mining and Security Opportunities in Indonesia

Indonesia is one of the world's largest producers of tin, coal and copper. Minerals and related products represent 19% of Indonesia's total exports, with gold being the largest revenue earner. This sector makes a huge contribution to the Indonesian economy, around 11.54% of total GDP.

As commodity prices fell during the Asian financial crisis, investment in Indonesia dropped with many major mining companies shelving their investment plans. The mining sector has bounced back in recent years, with growth driven by increasing gold prices and high demand for coal for power generation.

Indonesia has been subject to pressure from environmental groups because of illegal mining practices, land reclamation issues and un-clear regulations for foreign investment. However, there are plans for measures to attract more overseas investment.

The mining sector has bounced back in recent years, with growth driven by increasing gold prices and high demand for coal for power generation

Indonesia still remains at threat from terrorist attack as the bombings in July 2009 sadly illustrated. The attacks on the JW Marriott Hotel and the Ritz Carlton Hotel in Jakarta, which claimed the lives of 7 people and the discovery of a terrorist training camp in Aceh in late February 2010, serve as a reminder that terrorists still have the intent and capability to attack Western, including British interests in Indonesia.

Specialist anti-terrorist units within Police and military are geared up to combat this and this presents opportunities for UK companies to introduce new security equipment and training services which add value to existing products and processes.

As the world's largest archipelago covering some 17,000 islands, Indonesia is surrounded by the maritime boundaries of eight countries. This creates enormous issues concerning border security and leaves Indonesia vulnerable to transnational crimes (illegal fishing, smuggling, drug/human trafficking) and terrorist incursions. There is therefore potential opportunity for UK companies who can provide expertise and equipment which covers surveillance, communication and transmission devices, data gathering & analysis and capacity building & training.

Chapter 41: Opportunities in Indonesia Public and Private Sector

Public Sector

The Indonesian procurement mechanism within the defence & security sector can appear to be impenetrable at times. What is clear is that an effective local representation is essential in even getting this mechanism moving. A reputable intermediary with effective access into the relevant public bodies will ensure that your file does not gather dust and he can continue to present the benefits of the products and services to the decision-makers and gauge how serious they are.

The tendering process is the method of securing business with the Police and Military, unless the required product in question is of a highly sophisticated and technical nature where there is no obvious competition.

Most government tenders are published in the local media and on BAPPENAS' website: http://www.bappenas.go.id/. Having an effective and influential third party in place as a partner could pay real dividends in gaining access to the end users.

Culturally it is important to have face-to-face meetings whenever doing business and it is advisable to use the phone as the next best method as email is not used as much as in business dealings as in the UK.

There is an etiquette of arranging meetings with public officials in which the head of a department needs to be contacted by formal letter to request the meeting with the person you want to speak to, however, it is often the Local Representative who will arrange all necessary meetings whether formal or informal, and can also advise on business etiquette at the meeting.

The procurement mechanism for the Indonesian Police is similar to that of the Indonesian Military (TNI) in terms of export credit requirements and contracting.

Private Sector

The main route to market is through a distributor who has a presence in the country. Also, it is a legal requirement to have a local partner if you are supplying to the market. Alternatively, in the case of new build facilities in all sectors, the opportunities are in partnering with the Prime Contractor bidding on the projects.

Chapter 42: Education Opportunities in Indonesia

Indonesia's strong economy performance, coupled with steady young population growth, makes Indonesia too big a market to ignore.

A country report by Eurocham predicted that Indonesia will become the world's 5th-largest economy by 2050, behind Brazil, Russia, China and India.

The Education sector is on the Indonesian Government's Negative Investment List. This means there are very limited opportunities for foreign entities to invest in this sector. However, the Indonesian Government through the Ministry of National Education permits foreign universities to take part in twinning and dual degree programmes in Indonesia.

In January 2010, the British Council launched a major campaign to increase ties between UK and Indonesian institutions, including increasing bilateral engagement in higher education and improving quality, as well as maintaining the UK's position as a leader in international education."

The current education system in Indonesia is adapted from a system introduced by the former Dutch colonial administration, which is designed around 12 years of education in primary school, middle school and high school. The Ministry of National Education (Kementerian Pendidikan Nasional) is responsible for the education sector in Indonesia.

Education is among a few sectors that were included in the 2010 revision of the Indonesian Government's Negative Investment List. Foreign investors are now permitted to have a maximum 49% stake in a non-formal education entity. The higher education sector is regulated by Law Number 20/2003 concerning the National Education System. The law states that a foreign education provider must partner with a local education entity and employ local teaching staff.

With a solid core of wealthy Indonesians, a growing middle class with more money to spend on education and current reforms to lift educational standards, there are new opportunities for UK institutions to establish themselves in the market. The following opportunities are available:

1. Joint Research Programme and Institutional Linkages

Expansion of institutional partnerships, particularly for research in areas of global significance and shared concern, offer opportunities for UK Institutions to work with their Indonesian counterparts in improving educational performance and educating home-country students to an international standard.

2. Teacher development training programme

More than 54% of the total 2,603,650 teachers in Indonesia are under-qualified and still to obtain required qualification of Undergraduate Degree.

3. Vocational Education Programme

Differentiation of occupation in the developing economies requires secondary school graduates with varied skills, and good opportunities exist for providers of vocational education.

4. Corporate & Offshore programme

There is growing demand for programmes tailored to business requirements.

5. Cultural Exchanges & Study Abroad Programme

The UK remains an interesting destination for Indonesian students and the growing middle class have created an opportunity for UK institutions.

6. Tailored Training Programme

Opportunities exist across many areas of study, including finance, banking, oil & gas, manufacturing and agriculture.

7. TVET

In the development of its education system, including its vocational education system, Indonesia always had considerable support either from international donors or through the World Bank and Asian Development Bank. Currently several donors are supporting Indonesia with technical and financial aid in developing TVET.

8. English as Second Language

Indonesia offers a promising market for English as a second language. While English language is commonly taught in most high schools, most Indonesian students still attend an intensive English language preparation class before beginning their undergraduate studies.

Competitive Environment

Australia continues to be a market leader in education followed by USA and UK. In January 2010, the British Council launched a major educational campaign to increase ties between UK and Indonesian institutions, including increasing bilateral engagement in higher education, improving quality, as well as maintaining the UK's position as a leader in international education. In March 2010, the British Council invited an Indonesian delegation (rectors from top-ranked Indonesian universities) to visit the UK to attend the East Asia Regional Mission and the Going Global conference in London, as an opportunity to interact with senior leaders of UK universities and fellow East Asian participants. In November 2010, the British Council held an annual education exhibition in Jakarta.

UK and Indonesian universities with collaboration agreements include:

1. Air Service Training (Perth)
2. Bandung State Polytechnic
3. De Montfort University
4. Pelita Harapan University
5. Dundee University
6. Brawijaya University
7. Leeds Metropolitan University
8. Bandung School of Tourism
9. Leeds University
10. Muhammadiyah Malang University
11. Goldsmith, University of London
12. Institute Technology Bandung
13. Northumbria University
14. Bina Nusantara University
15. Oxford Centre for Islamic Studies
16. Gadjah Mada University
17. Sheffield Hallam University
18. Bina Nusantara University
19. Sheffield Hallam University
20. Trisakti University
21. University of Essex, University of Bedfordshire, and University of Gloucestershire
22. Indonesia Islamic University
23. University of Glasgow
24. University of Indonesia
25. University of Newcastle
26. Bogor Agriculture Institute
27. University of Newcastle

28. Institute Technology Sepuluh Nopember
29. University of Newcastle
30. University of Indonesia
31. University of Newcastle
32. Institute Technology Sepuluh Nopember
33. University of Portsmouth
34. Petra Christian University

Chapter 43: Food and Drink Opportunities in Indonesia

Indonesia's economy, at USD 700 billion, is the largest in South East Asia, one of the most rapidly growing regions in the world. The country has experienced strong economic expansion over the past years, with growth recorded at a respectable 4.5% and 6% in 2009 and 2010 respectively. Medium-term economic growth is expected to reach 7%, signalling the biggest economy in South East Asia is inching closer towards the original BRIC countries (Brazil, Russia, India, and China).

As the world's fourth most populous nation, Indonesia is home to more than 240 million people, largely centred in urban areas. At least 35 million of the population representing a market greater in size than Australia, New Zealand and Singapore combined; comprise the targeted middle to upper segments for imported products.

Demand for food, beverage, cosmetics, pharmaceuticals, household and other consumer products have been fuelled by the country's increasing middle class. The food and beverage industry in particular, has recorded rapid growth and is expected to grow by approximately 20% over the next 5 years.

A vast array of imported food and beverage products have been widely accepted by the Indonesian market, particularly amongst the middle-upper segments, largely because foreign brands are perceived to be of higher quality than those produced locally.

Products that are expected to record the highest growth include:

1. Dairy Products

Indonesia is currently the sixth largest dairy market in Asia-Pacific, with an expected CAGR growth of 5-10% from 2009 – 2014. Imported milk products supply a majority of the market demand, dominated by liquid ready-to-drink (UHT) milk, sweetened condensed milk, and powdered milk.

2. Organic & Health Products

Increased health awareness has driven demand for healthy / 'speciality' products (wheat-free, gluten free, dairy free, vegan, organic, etc), largely available at leading supermarket chains and specialized stores. The Ministry of Agriculture has estimated that there are potentially 15 million consumers who are prepared to pay for such products.

3. Confectionary & Snacks

Indonesia's confectionary and snack food industry has successfully targeted its core demographic, an estimated 82 million Indonesian children and teenagers. Snacking is a fundamental part of life in Indonesia and the snack food industry is expected to record an annual growth rate of 20% over the next five years.

4. Fresh Fruits

Indonesia consumes over 35 kg of fruits per capita, and a significant demand for imported fruits and vegetables is driven by urban consumers demanding a wider range of premium and quality produce. Primarily marketed to the middle-upper segments, they are often re-distributed at conventional supermarkets and retail outlets to appeal to the middle-low segments.

5. Processed and Frozen Foods

Changing urban lifestyles and the growth in the number of working mothers have increased demand for processed-food products, particularly: frozen French fries, frozen and canned vegetables, breakfast cereals, baby food, dressings, sauces, seasonings, etc. Refrigerated frozen foods such as frozen pizza, frozen meats, delicatessen meats and speciality fruits are also increasingly favoured by the upper segments of the market.

6. Functional Beverages & Ingredients

Although milk and dairy based beverages remain the leading functional beverages for people of all age groups in the country, there has been increasing demand for nutrition and supplement drinks, along with flavoured tea and juice drinks that contain vitamins, minerals, natural sugars, fibres, etc. The functional beverages market is expected to record a CAGR of almost 10% over the next 5 years. As the country's domestic ingredients industry is not yet able to service market demand, manufacturers rely heavily greatly on imported functional ingredients.

7. Ready-to-Drink Coffee

Indonesia has a strong coffee drinking culture and is currently the largest coffee consumption market in South East Asia. Lifestyle changes and increased standards of living have resulted in demand for ready-to-drink (instant) coffee and high-end coffee outlets. Ready-to-drink coffee, especially popular amongst younger consumers, is expected to record a CAGR of 14% over the next 5 years.

To take advantage of the opportunities available, it is crucial that companies:

1. Appoint the right business partner (after undertaking due diligence work)
2. Visit the market on a regular basis (face-to-face contact and the development of relationships is critical to business success)
3. Prepare comprehensive information packs profiling your company, product specifications, pricing and terms of payment.
4. Participate in major trade exhibitions to showcase products/ services to relevant audience/ buyers.

Characteristics of the Market

According to latest data from the country's Central Statistical Bureau, the average Indonesian dedicates 53% of their total income to food and beverage consumption. This increases markedly during major festive occasions, including: Ramadhan (the month-long Muslim fasting period), Lebaran (Muslim celebration at the end of Ramadhan), Chinese New Year, and several Western celebrations which have become increasingly popular in the country, particularly Christmas and Valentine's Day. Even though food and beverage purchases at traditional retail outlets still record dominance, modern retailers and a range of high-end speciality food stores, are increasingly gaining popularity amongst the middle to upper segments.

Western lifestyle influences have driven choices for food and beverage purchases, and a majority of the middle-upper income families are less price sensitive, opting for gourmet and imported items. Key Methods of Doing Business Significant reforms to improve the ease of doing business in the Indonesia have been implemented, making the country an attractive investment and business market for UK companies. Product registration, however, can still prove to be lengthy, bureaucratic, and costly. Foreign food and beverage importers commonly enter the market through partnerships with distributors and/or agents.

Distributors and agents are able to provide the much-needed network to achieve extensive local coverage, distributing the products directly to retailers, the food service industry and other stakeholders in the industry.

As of September 2010, the National Agency of Food & Drug Control (BPOM) has also implemented a requirement for all food and non-food products circulating in the country to carry labelling in Indonesian, setting out details of ingredients utilized, an expiration date determined by the Ministry of

Health, and storage and preparation instructions when applicable.

"Halal" certification is not mandatory for all food products, however, given almost 90% of the population is Muslim, "Halal" remains a very significant aspect. Obtaining "Halal" certification is often recommended, and it is essential to have an in-depth understanding of the procedures and requirements of attaining "Halal" certificates for food and beverage products entering the market.

Chapter 44: Financial Services Opportunities in Indonesia

Indonesia is an open market for the financial services sector with huge potential growth in banking both conventional and Islamic banking, insurance particularly life segment and capital market.

Indonesia's economic growth continues to be strong at 6.5% in 2011 and predicted to reach 6.1%-6.3%% in 2012, and is South East Asia's largest economy.

There are 122 banks with more than 13,000 branches in Indonesia. These consist of state-owned banks, local private banks (foreign exchange and non-foreign exchange licensed banks), foreign banks and the regional development banks.

Bank Indonesia (Central Bank) has the authority to issue policy rules and regulations. In October 2011, Indonesia's Parliament passed long-awaited law to establish a financial services regulator (OJK) which will have supervisory and regulatory oversight of banks, NBFIs and financial markets. The OJK is expected to start operating in 2013.

Apart from Bank Indonesia, there are several other regulatory bodies which have influence over the banking system. The Indonesian Capital Market and Financial Institution Agency (BAPEPAM-LK) and Indonesia Stock Exchange also have a significant regulatory role, particularly in relation to the settlement of marketable securities and related accounts.

Foreign banks can establish a new bank, open a local branch or buy into existing local banks with up to 99% foreign ownership limit.

Continuous growth of middle class in recent years offers huge opportunities for priority banking product.

Banks are increasingly focusing on providing better services and product innovation to their customers. Consequently, many banks continue to invest in IT-based banking systems and software.

Considering the size of the Muslim population in Indonesia and the growth of the Islamic banking sector over the past 5 years, strategic investment and partnerships are to be fund in expanding the product base that Sharia banks are able to offer to customers. Limited knowledge of more sophisticated banking products presents collaboration opportunities.

There are various methods of entry into Indonesia's Banking Sector:
1. Purchase of shares in banking entities.
2. Acquiring an existing bank.
3. Opening up a branch of a foreign bank.
4. Establishing a new bank.
5. Investing in Islamic banks.

Chapter 45: Ports Sector Opportunities in Indonesia

Ports are relatively small compared to other countries in South East Asia and require improvements. This is of particular concern as sea transportation is a vital aspect of the country's trading infrastructure carrying over 90% of internationally traded goods.

There are hundreds of small ports throughout Indonesia. Of these, 111 are commercial ports operated by state-owned companies, PT Pelindo I, II, III and IV while only 11 are container ports.

Indonesia lacks large scale ports capable of receiving trans-oceanic vessels and the limited port capacity has created a highly inefficient system. As a result, much of Indonesia's cargo has to go through Malaysia and Singapore. High transaction costs due to port inefficiencies, congestion and border transactions are one of the largest obstacles that prevent Indonesian firm and consumers reaping the full advantage of growing global international trade linkages.

Jakarta's Tanjung Priok port (through which 70% of Indonesia's container exports and imports pass) is the main international gateway and a major gateway for domestic trade. Limited capacities, congestion and low level of productivity at the port hamper exports and the domestic distribution of products. In 2010, the port handled 4.6 million TEUs.

The need to upgrade facilities is recognised by the government and a new drive is underway as part of the national infrastructure development master plan. New ports are being planned to relieve some of the congestion.

The Master Plan includes explicitly the urgent need for upgrading of Tanjung Priok port. The decision to develop Kalibaru container port worth IDR 11.7 trillion (approximately US$ 1.3 billion), near Tanjung Priok is expected in early February 2012. The new container port will ease off some of the pressure from Tanjung Priok. The proposed Kalibaru container terminal will have a capacity of up to 6.5 million TEUs as well as host an oil & gas terminal.

Further upgrade plans under PT Pelindo I, II, III and IV are underway, including capacity expansion of Tanjung Priok by 1.7 million TEUs, a new terminal in Sorong (Papua), Cimalaya (West Java), a new port in Lamong Bay (Surabaya, East Java).

Presidential Regulation No. 54/2010 which came into effect on 1 January, 2011 governs, among others, procurements by ministries, state-owned enterprises, funded in part or entirely from domestic loans or grants received by the government, financed in part or entirely from international loans or grants.

Public tender is the standard method of procurement. In all public tenders, information is published on the procuring entity's website, the formal notice boards, increasingly, the Electronic Procurement Service portals.

Foreign companies are allowed to bid in cooperation with a national company (unless no national company has the ability to provide the goods or services requested) and only on bids that exceed a certain threshold e.g. IDR 100 billion (approximately US$ 10 million) for construction services.

Most companies use the website of National Public Procurement Office and printed media as a source of information about calls for tenders.

Chapter 46: Overseas Business Risk - Indonesia

Political and Economic

Overall the political situation in Indonesia is stable. The country has gone through a remarkable transformation over the last 10 years from an authoritarian regime to one of the most free societies in south east Asia. See Freedomhouse.org for details. The transition was turbulent; involving the Asian financial crisis, the fall of a leader who had ruled for 32 years, an overhaul for the political and legislative frame-works, serious ethnic and religious conflict and the devastating 2004 tsunami.

Indonesia has now developed into the third largest democracy in the world with the first direct elections for President being held in 2004. A comprehensive push for decentralisation has seen much power transferred to the regions. President Bambang Yudhoyono became Indonesia's first ever democratically re-elected president with 60% of the vote. He was inaugurated for his second term on 20 October 2009. The overall human rights situation has improved significantly over the last 20 years. However there are ongoing allegations of human rights abuses in Papua and elsewhere in Indonesia. We raise credible reports with the Indonesian authorities. The Indonesian government has made real progress in tackling terrorism since the devastating bomb attacks in Bali in 2002 and subsequent bombings, but the threat of terrorism remains; please refer to the FCO Travel Advice for details.

The justice system in Indonesia has a reputation for slowness and inefficiency and is regarded as a significant problem by many British companies.

Bribery and Corruption

Bribery is illegal in Indonesia and the Government is fully committed to tackling all forms of corruption. In 2002, a Corruption Eradication Commission (KPK) was established to investigate and prosecute alleged offenders and an increasing number of high level officials and businessmen have been taken to court. Public sentiment towards corruption has changed and Indonesians are increasingly less tolerant of corruption.

Despite these efforts, Indonesia ranked 110th in the 2010 Transparency International's corruption perception index (CPI) barely an improvement on the previous year, and corruption remains a regular feature of business life. Companies considering business partnerships should carry out due diligence prior to selecting partners as a means to managing the risk of being affected by fraud or corruption carried out by a third party.

Visit the Business Anti-Corruption portal page providing advice and guidance about corruption in Indonesia and some basic effective procedures you can establish to protect your company from them.

Terrorism Threat

The Indonesian National Police have been very successful in disrupting and tracking down suspected terrorists. However, a high threat from terrorism persists.

The nature of the terrorism threat in Indonesian continues to evolve, having mutated from Jema'ah Islamiyah (JI) being commonly regarded as the principal threat to Western interests to the emergence of JI-affiliated and offshoot groups as well as autonomous militant groups. Considered a regional terrorist organisation, Jema'ah Islamiyah is now mainly active in Indonesia and the southern Philippines. Its aim remains to create a unified Islamic state across the region.

Jema'ah Islamiyah and its offshoots are believed to have been responsible for several high-profile attacks, including the bombings of nightclubs and bars in Bali (2002), the JW Marriott Hotel in Jakarta (2003), the Australian Embassy in Jakarta (2004) and three restaurants in Bali (2005).

Since 2002, Indonesian law enforcement counter terrorism operations have arrested over 500 individuals, severely weakening terrorist networks in Indonesia. However, in the last 12 months, many analysts believe that terrorist networks in the country appear to have grown in sophistication and were larger in number and geographical reach than previously believed.

The 17 July 2009 attacks on the JW Marriott Hotel and the Ritz Carlton Hotel in Jakarta, which claimed the lives of 7 people, serve as a reminder that terrorists still have the intent and capability to attack Western, including British interests in Indonesia. The Indonesian National Police counter terrorism response to the attacks led to a number of arrests and deaths, including Noordin Muhammad Top, the leader of a JI splinter group held responsible for many of the terrorist bombings in Indonesia since 2002.

The UK works with Indonesia within international law to prevent terrorist attacks, encouraging law enforcement activities to track down and prosecute those who are responsible. This work also aims to provide better security against attacks and improve the response to incidents.

Businessmen should be aware that there has been a marked increase in the fraudulent use of stolen or cloned credit cards to purchase goods or services from the UK and elsewhere through the internet. There has also been an increase in the number of bogus web-sites offering products from Indonesia. For such transactions, it is important to first ensure that the companies are legitimate before sending any payment. The age-old maxim holds: "if it sounds too good to be true, it probably is".

Intellectual Property

Indonesia is a member of the World Intellectual Property Organisation and a party to the Paris Convention for the protection of intellectual property. It is also a signatory of the General Agreements on Tariffs and Trade (GATT) and to its subsidiary agreement, GATS. It recognises the importance of intellectual property protection, and has drawn up a number of bills increasing the protection of intellectual property rights. Indonesia has laws covering patents, copyrights (Law No 19 of 2002) and trademarks. It should be noted however that local implementation remains weak; there is a lack of capacity and enforcement of regulations and this also applies to border controls. British and foreign companies operating in the market have been affected by a number of IP issues including Trade Mark Squatters, Trade Mark Registration Squatters and Counterfeiting.

We have no evidence of organised crime affecting foreign companies doing business with Indonesia.

Chapter 47: Conclusion

Indonesia is the biggest economy in Southeast Asia ($700 billion), is in the midst of a boom driven by consumption and natural resource exports. But the Indonesian financial markets are already feeling the ill-effect of the global downturn. Can the boom last in the face of a global double-dip? We see the risks as significant, but manageable.

A high-growth story...

Indonesia's growth is driven by two key factors: demographics (and consumption) and natural resources. Some two-thirds of the population is in the productive age of 15-64, with a median age of 28. On the back of this, the middle class is growing rapidly. Our own estimate, based on Nielsen's criteria of $7,000 per capita expenditure, put the figure at 45 million, up from 35 million two years ago. Such growth will change the market landscape with more people spending less on basic necessities and more on higher-end consumer goods. Private consumption, at 56% of GDP, has already driven the economy for the past decade.

Natural resources contributed 57% to GDP in 2010. These include oil and gas, minerals, palm oil, base metal, and rubber. Indonesia is now the largest exporter of palm oil and thermal coal, mostly to China, India, and Japan. The country's share of global exports in these two commodities increased from 5%

each in 1995 to 15% for coal in 2009 and more than 20% for palm oil.

For the moment the economy is moving forward strongly, with an estimated 2011 growth rate of 6.4% and 6.7% in 2012. But troubles in the world economy have already send modest shockwaves through the Indonesian financial markets, with the rupiah down 5% since the beginning of September and the Jakarta stock exchange by about 17%, and attention is focusing on the extent to which the economy more generally is vulnerable to external forces. A variety of factors are cited as likely to constrain growth and investor confidence. What are these vulnerabilities and what impact might they have?

Short-term risks, long-term opportunities

The 2014 presidential election is already intruding into scenario planning. The current front-runners to succeed President Yudhayana have poor reformist credentials, although the picture could well change significantly before then. The boom is, however, unlikely to end in 2014, whoever is elected, as economic policies do not tend to change significantly or suddenly. Politicians of different parties will continue to rely on the same Western-educated pool of economists. But 2014 will increasingly inject uncertainty into the climate.

The current global market turmoil is inevitably focusing attention on Indonesia's susceptibility to global financial flows. The country is sufficiently large (liquid) and open to attract "hot" money which makes her markets and currency more volatile than others in the region, and therefore susceptible to contagion. That said, Indonesia's real economy is relatively isolated from the small financial hub in Jakarta, and the government and firms are far less reliant on foreign financing than they were before 1997. The banks are now prudently managed - a legacy of that crisis. In the short term, the financial market will continue to be small, niche, and volatile.

The lack of infrastructure (particularly transport) slows growth, creates bottlenecks and inflation. Public-private partnerships are starting to be piloted, although only two projects have been approved so far. In the next five years, as consumption and production grow without the corresponding transport and energy infrastructure in place, this infrastructure deficit will result in higher structural inflation and, subsequently, slower growth. But, the lack of infrastructure also presents a major investment opportunity for foreign businesses.

The economy needs also to shift away from natural resource dependence. The government's Economic Master Plan emphasises more value-added manufacturing and limitation of raw materials exports. Businesses are sceptical but there are indeed signs that the economy is becoming more diversified. Manufacturing is recovering for the first time in a decade and a half; transportation and communications are the fastest growing sub-sectors; and investors are shifting from portfolio to real sector investments. Investors in manufacturing are not only coming from Indonesia's traditional sources (Japan,

Singapore, the US), but also from China, where wages are now more expensive than Indonesia's.

The Indonesian market is still hampered by regulatory barriers and corruption. It is, however, still possible for foreign investors to navigate the barriers without resorting to bribery. This need not put UK firms at a competitive disadvantage, especially since UK and EU goods are not competing with lower-end manufacturing products from other parts of Asia. Regulatory and legal uncertainty, however, remain a significant risk to business, and we know of cases where foreign companies are delaying decisions on investment in the face of such uncertainty, e.g. in the oil and gas and banking sectors.

Although corruption is deeply ingrained, it is increasingly out of touch with sentiment among the young and the middle classes. Indonesia is the world's second-largest market for Facebook, and the third-largest for Twitter. These educated middle classes are aware of the income inequalities and corruption and are increasingly able to express and network this sentiment. This, in time, will feed into the ballot box.

This is not a market for the faint-hearted. Investing in the country requires patience, perseverance, a presence on the ground (or at least frequent visits), and relationship building (beyond business). Churchill Mining's experience (reported in The Economist at is a classic example of the type of difficulties that foreign investors can encounter. But, many judge the rewards to be worth the risks: the biggest company by revenue in Indonesia is British-owned (Jardines).

An adequate understanding of the cultural environment is essential in order to successful undertake business in Indonesia. Practical day-to-day business requires entry into a multiplicity of human interactions, all of which have some basis in culture. Even before language, an understanding of cultural assumptions is fundamental to proper communication, which in turn is fundamental to good business. Stories of cultural collisions and misunderstandings of Westerners in Indonesia can make for entertaining anecdotes, but in business, mistakes due to such miscommunication can be quite expensive.

Time spent acquiring knowledge about Indonesian's social and cultural environment is not time wasted; it is as important as studying the economic climate or researching a business plan. A measure of cultural knowledge will greatly assist the Westerner in dealing with and accommodating the significant cultural differences that exist in Indonesia to achieve successful business outcomes.

Good Luck!

Made in the USA
Middletown, DE
07 January 2016